LIVE
AFTER DEATH

TPJ VAN DER WALT

Freedom in the Kingdom 2017

 A catalogue record for this book is available from the National Library of Australia

Copyright © 2017 TPJ Van Der Walt

All rights reserved worldwide.

No part of the book may be copied or changed in any format, sold, or used in a way other than what is outlined in this book, under any circumstances, without the prior written permission of the publisher.

Publisher:
Inspiring Publishers
P.O. Box 159, Calwell, ACT Australia 2905
Email: publishaspg@gmail.com
http://www.inspiringpublishers.com

National Library of Australia Cataloguing-in-Publication entry

Author: Walt, TPJ Van Der.

Title: **LIVE AFTER DEATH**/*TPJ Van Der Walt*.

ISBN: 9780648155768 (pbk)

Introduction

*My **ULTIMATE** prayer to **GOD*** is that there are enough ***BIBLE*** references in this book and not just empty words which can easily mislead people and the SPIRIT of ***GOD*** allow doing a complete work, and more souls and names written into the book of life. The only *LIVING GOD* and *CREATOR*. ***HIS** SPIRIT* allowed me a second chance to present ***HIS*** work to many people not knowing ***HIM***, or none active Christians and to give labourers in his work material to lead more to ***HIS** Kingdom*. "Now my experience on a normal Friday morning after shower, dressed, serial and only had to brush my teeth and instantly had a blackout and can't remember how I got to the side of my bed with a excessively high hart beat. I hit myself on the chest and loudly cried with my hands up in the air to ***GOD*** to help me. I checked on my watch with my hand on my chest counting 57 beats per 15 seconds continuing for a period. It lasted precisely 12 minutes. The SPIRIT of ***GOD*** inspired me to write twelve chapters to distribute to as many people over the globe".

Inspired by:
TPJ Van Der Walt

Contents

Chapter 1: How should I start?..7

Chapter 2: Five minutes after death of a believer..................... 42

Chapter 3: Five minutes after death of a none believer.......... 55

Chapter 4: The first resurrection 70

Chapter 5: Glorified bodies of the righteous 83

Chapter 6: Problems with death texting..................................... 97

Chapter 7: The judgement-seat of JESUS.................................. 111

Chapter 8: White throne judgement of GOD.......................... 124

Chapter 9: Glory of the new earth 138

Chapter 10: The new Jerusalem – the new GOD CITY 150

Chapter 11: How does a child of GOD DIE? 162

Chapter 12: What should I do now and
how should I stay..174

Chapter 1
How should I start?

*There is **twelve** important things you should do; the moment you made the decision to accept **JESUS** and **GOD** through the **HOLY SPIRIT** as your personal saviour. The general prayer taught to you when you repent: ask **CHRIST** to forgive you from all your sins, and that you accept **HIM** as your personal saviour, and commit yourself to accept **HIM** as your **GOD**, and that you will be a child of **GOD** and praise him with your life, and ask **GOD** to renew your mind to never turn back to your old week ways and not to sin. Through the voice of the **HOLY SPIRIT** always guiding us and warn us of the wrong things. The voice is actually called your conscious. From the start of your growing process you were told to change your ways, like to change your friends and try to get reborn Christian friends to give you guidance. Then after you became more mature in **GOD**, then return to your old friends to try and win them for **CHRIST**.*

You can grow in faith by joining a Christian church. An important thought is to join in with a church which believes in **GOD** the **FATHER**, **SON** and **HOLY SPIRIT**. In such a church you will meet true Christians who can lead and assist you, guide you to hear **GOD'S** voice and to grow in **HIS** calling and work. If unknown to you the moment you give your life to **GOD** the ultimate happens for the first time in your life, when you use your spirit, soul and body as a unit. Rom 8:10-39 *"And if Christ is in you, the body is dead because of sin, but the Spirit is life because of righteousness. But if the Spirit of Him who raised Jesus from the dead dwells in you, He who raised Christ from the dead will also give life to your mortal bodies through His Spirit who dwells in you."* Say we can split up the three for argument: **Firstly** your "**Spirit**" is eternal and will be there forever and is your only communication portal to **GOD**.

Gal 5:25 *"If we live in the Spirit, let us also walk in the Spirit."* **Secondly** your "**Soul**": will also live forever and is there for **GOD'S** use only.

This is a draw full of peoples experience only, no wonder we read of people who wrote of their dreams, visions of how **JESUS** took them to see hell; those people can remember one another, but can't communicate with **GOD** from hell.

Thirdly your "**Body**": When you as a new born baby living on earth, you are pretty, perfect and good. When you are a grownup you should understand that you have to live for **GOD**. Remember not living for **GOD** after death your spirit and body burns in hell and your soul forever lost with the devil. We read in Rom 12:2 *"And do not be conformed to this world, but be transformed by the renewing of your mind, that you may prove* *what is that good and acceptable and perfect will of God."* Now not all have the same gifts and only known through **GOD'S SPIRIT** when you start in his work. There are many things we need to know and learn to walk **GOD'S** way. You truthfully come to a total stop and came to this point looking up and see the "**CROSS**" then turn from the broad road to follow **JESUS** on the narrow way. We read in Gal 2:20 *"I have been crucified with Christ; it is no longer I who live, but Christ lives in me; and the life which I now live in the flesh I live by faith in the Son of God, who loved me and gave Himself for me."*

You can see now the first step is to repent and that means return to you maker, the creator of all and the human being. There is only one living **GOD** and he was there from the beginning.

We read in Joh 1:1-4 *"In the beginning was the WORD, and the WORD was with God, and the word was God."* Continue to read up to verse 4, this section gives you a good insight that **GOD** who was always there and your planner from the beginning and therefore the **BIBLE** is the only given guide by **GOD** to teach us in truth from the beginning of existence to the end, as you will follow through the rest of the following chapters.

Also confirmed by Peter in 1 Pet 1:23 and 25. Verse 23 *"having been born again, not of corruptible seed but incorruptible, through the word of God which lives and abides forever,"*

Verse 25 *"having been born again, not of corruptible seed but incorruptible, through the word of God which lives and abides forever, But the word of the LORD endures forever. Now this is the word which by the gospel was preached to you."*

Now that we know who **GOD** is, in the following chapters we will learn who **JESUS** and **GOD'S SPIRIT** are and will learn that they are the light of the world. There are not enough pages to describe **GOD** and **HIS** might, you know how gigantic **GOD** is to create all: just think of the sky and the earth one of the small planets **GOD** created which we have the privilege to know and live to learn of **GOD'S** creation. We are a million times smaller than earth and still **GOD** deals with us and call us his child. Also life gives life to the smallest organism which is million times smaller than us. With this I need to say don't underestimate **GOD'S** almighty and do not play with **GOD**. In the following chapters I will mention a couple of things that **GOD** has proven to man what **HE** did to people who sinned against **HIM** or being against **HIM**. The word sin is repeated 234 times in the **BIBLE**. How do we know who has the right to forgive sins? We read of a couple places in the **WORD** when **JESUS** was on earth and said: *"Your sins are forgiven"* like in Joh 8:11 *"She said, No one, Lord. And Jesus said to her, neither do I condemn you; go and sin no more."* You see **JESUS** has the power.

In one of my previous modules I have written about sins, you can learn all about sins written in the **BIBLE**. You may request this module and study it thoroughly. The word repent is written down 151 times in the **BIBLE**, my module about repent is also available on request. Repent means: Stop in your tracks of your wrong ways of sin and completely turn away from those and turn to **GOD** and **HIS** ways and learn the **GODHEAD** and **HIS** way.

You learn **GOD'S** way, the guidance of the **HOLY SPIRIT** the moment you repent and start talking to **GOD** and learn **HIS** voice in your head.

At this moment I need to tell you it isn't only the believers **GOD** speaks to but all human beings. The reason **GOD** created the human race is to worship and praise **HIM** and **HE** doesn't want anybody get lost and casted into hell. Because **HE** is the creator who should be worshipped alone and **HE** is the only truth and nothing happens without being through **HIM**. **GOD** gives life. **HE** is the truth and way. In the following chapters you will realise there is no liars in heaven. Now you know you will not enter heaven with your wrong ways and sins.

You notice the reason why preachers teach you the moment you repent, you ask GOD to clench you and wash you as white as snow and to live in you to prepare you for **HIS** kingdom. Eternal life with **HIM**, in truth and glory. The choice to follow **JESUS** is the easiest decision by far and who prefers to be ugly full of sins and burning eternally in hell with the corrupted one. Remember as heaven is real the hell is real too. To make a promise to **GOD** at your repentance means to accept **HIM** as your personal saviour and that you accept **HIM** as your **GOD** who teaches you **HIS** way. The **WORD** says the sin lies at your door. We read in Gen 4:7 *"If you do well, will you not be accepted? And if you do not do well, sin lies at the door. And its desire is for you, but you should rule over it."*

The **second** thing we learn at repentance is to pray, like the person who led you to **GOD** taught you. You pray and ask **GOD** to accept you and to forgive all your sins. **JESUS** taught us how to pray in Mat 6:9-13 verse 9 pray like this:

"Our Father in heaven
Hallowed be your name.
Your kingdom come.
Your will be done on earth as it is in heaven.
Give us this day our daily bread.
And forgive us our debts,
As we forgive our debtors. And do not lead us into temptation,
But deliver us from the evil one.
For Yours is the kingdom and the power and the glory forever.
Amen."

We are going to take a moment and work through the prayer **JESUS** taught us and realise a bit of the **GODHEAD** discovery **JESUS** gave us in **HIS** prayer and realise that this person **JESUS** is actually **GOD** telling us how we should praise **HIM** because **HE** knows, **HE** is the creator who knows the human being.

A prayer like this is actually the only way to speak and communicate to **GOD** to strengthen and know surely there is a living **GOD** and that **HE** will answer us through his **HOLY SPIRIT**. You should also work through The Beatitudes in Mat 5, 6 and 7 chapters and also discover this is **GOD** giving us **HIS KINGDOM** preaching through **JESUS** on earth. As newborn Christian you need to start to gain knowledge of the **HEAVENLY FATHER**.

Looking at the first part of **JESUS'S** prayer we learn in Mat 6:9 *"Our Father in heaven"* This is our acknowledgement that **GOD** exists and we only praise **HIM**. We have to humiliate and humble ourselves before **GOD** and tell our **HEAVENLY FATHER** how great and worthy **HE** is to be praised. And that **HE** is the creator of heaven and earth. And that **GOD** gives us the next breath of life and that **HE** alone is worthy to be with, forever.

"Hallowed be Your name" **GOD** is **HOLY** and not like the earthly gods and statues. We praise **HIM** and give **HIM** all the glory as we read in 1 Cron 16:29 says: *"Give to the LORD the glory due His name;"* We have to kneel and bow before **GOD** who gives us life. When we pray we are privilege to speak to **GOD** our creator. According to John 4:24 *"God is SPIRIT, and those who worship HIM must worship in spirit and truth"* With all truth because **HE** is the reason for your existence.

"Your kingdom come" We pray for reality about the end time as I will describe it in later chapters, and ask **HIM** for insight thereof and ask **HIM** to come soonest. We read in Mat 18: 18 and 19. 18*"Assuredly, I say to you, whatever you bind on earth will be bound in heaven, and whatever you loose on earth will be loosed in heaven. 19 Again I say to you that if two of you agree on earth concerning anything that they ask, it will be done for them by My Father in heaven."* So **JESUS** gives his disciples earthly rights and power to bind and unbined things like your church, your preacher or family.

"Your will be done on earth as it is in heaven;" We pray that **HIS** will be done not the evil ones under we as human beings

suffer with temptations like sins, slavery of evil works and pray practice. We pray and secure our bond with **GOD** and ask **HIM** support to keep us from it as he said:

"Your will be done on earth as it is in heaven" We admit that **HE** is the light and truth we channel our existence through and believe non truth won't enter in heaven. And admit that the devil always been the liar and will end in hell. And because we know that he is **GOD** and knows us. Our **GOD** is love and merciful. Do not be afraid of **HIS** will in our live. Do you believe **GOD** will hurt his children? **GOD** will provide more than what your parents ever given you. Ask **GOD** then **HIS** will in your live, your church, your family and friends.

Further *"Give us this day our daily bread"* we discovered in The Beatitudes that **GOD** provides all to us where **HE** says: *"why do you concern about tomorrow"* and *"you are worth more than"* but you actually need to ask **GOD** to provide you with food and cloth you. **GOD** wants you to ask **HIM** for all through prayer. This part of the prayer is the part where you ask **GOD** what you need but not your desires, always praise **GOD** for what **HE** gives us. Mat 10:31 *"Do not fear therefore; you are of more value than many sparrows."* Praise **GOD** always for what he gives you.

Then *"And forgive us our debts,"* we ask **GOD** to forgive us of all our sins. In another scripture the **BIBLE** says:

"All sinned and withhold us the kingdom of **GOD**". We always have to pray forgiveness of our sins but remember the promise you just made to **GOD** to accept **HIM** and to turn back from sin. Sometimes it is difficult to forgive but you have to. It is important to be clean and without sin when you near **GOD** in prayer, you got to be cleansed coming before **GOD** your **CREATOR**, to prevent an honest prayer request to be rejected by your **CREATOR**. Ps 119:11 says: *"Your word I have hidden in my heart, that I might not sin against You."* Always ask **GOD** to forgive you and to forgive your debtors who sinned against you or against **GOD**. And learn to forgive thy neighbour even before they sin against you, with prayer prevention of bad things and temptation towards you.

Further *"As we forgive our debtors"*. How many times are we sinning against others and others against us and never asked for forgiveness.

No forgiveness brings you to a stop as sinner and can't get forgiveness until you receive forgiveness. So **GOD** wants us to immediately forgive or to ask forgiveness. Remember when **JESUS** wrote on the ground when the Pharisees brought the lady to **JESUS** for **HIS** advice and wanted to stone her for her sins, **JESUS** said: " Joh 8:7 *So when they continued asking Him, He raised Himself up and said to them, "He who is without sin among you, let him throw a stone at her first."* We all make mistakes and have to admit to it and forgive to continue in **GOD'S** will. We have to pray that **GOD** to help us with our weaknesses and prevent you to fall. Remember temptation is not a sin, **JESUS** himself was tempted on earth it only becomes sin when you sin. Ask **FATHER** to help you to keep you safe from temptation.

With *"And do not lead us into temptation"* we ask **GOD** that the devil does not tempt us with sin.

Following *"But deliver us from the evil one"* sins are evil as the **WORD** says: Directly lit from hell by the tongue committed to start sins. You can also request my module about the tongue.

Further *"For Yours is the kingdom and the power and the glory forever "*. The same as the beginning of this prayer we praise and glorify **HIS NAME**.

In the following chapters I explain the **GODHEAD** and the eternity. Prayer is your strength and built up to **GOD**. Your worship is your greeting to **GOD** to have free time with **FATHER** because the times you pray and praise **HIM** becomes less as live continues. The more you speak to **GOD** the more the **HOLY SPIRIT** gives you knowledge to grow in **GOD'S** work and know **GOD**. Remember **JESUS** said if you only had faith the size of a mustard seed you would say to the mountain to move. Let us read Luk 17:6 *"So the Lord said, "If you have faith as a mustard seed, you can say to this mulberry tree, 'Be pulled up by the roots and be planted in the sea,' and it would obey you."* Also Mat 17:20 *"So Jesus said to them, Because of your unbelief; for assuredly, I say to you, if you have faith as a mustard seed, you will say to this mountain, 'Move from here to there,' and it will move; and nothing will be impossible for you."*

And Jam 1:6 *"But let him ask in faith, with no doubting, for he who doubts is like a wave of the sea driven and tossed by the wind."*

This brings us to the **third** part, how do you know you are now a child of **GOD**? Jona 1:12 *"And he said to them, Pick me up and throw me into the sea; then the sea will become calm for you. For I know that this great tempest is because of me."* and in Rom 8:14 *"For as many as are led by the Spirit of God, these are sons of God."* So we also see the inverse in Rom 9:8 *"That is, those who are the children of the flesh, these are not the children of God; but the children of the promise are counted as the seed."* And also where **GOD'S** anger is against the non believer. We read in Col 3:16 *"Let the word of Christ dwell in you richly in all wisdom, teaching and admonishing one another in psalms and hymns and spiritual songs, singing with grace in your hearts to the Lord."* Then also in Mat 5:9 *"Blessed are the peacemakers, for they shall be called sons of God."*

Now Rom 8:16 *"The Spirit Himself bears witness with our spirit that we are children of God,"* In 1 Joh 5:2 *"By this we know that we love the children of God, when we love God and keep His commandments."* 1 Joh 3:10 *"In this the children of God and the children of the devil are manifest: Whoever does not practice righteousness is not of God, nor is he who does not love his brother."* Rom 8:21 *"because the creation itself also will be delivered from the bondage of corruption into the glorious liberty of the children of God."* The answer is easy, in the **OLD TESTAMENT** we learn that the priest had to enter for your sins and offer on your behalf.

Then **GOD** sent **JESUS** to come and teach us about **GOD** and to come and give **HIS** life for our sins. This is the only way to purify you from sin, and to believe in **JESUS'S** blood flowing for you and me on the cross. Also as a new borne I confirm with prayer. "My personal **SAVIOUR**". I admit that **JESUS** died for me. In the **OLD TESTAMENT** it says nothing happens unless it is written in **GOD'S WORD**. The **NEW TESTAMENT** from the four gospels describes **JESUS** and the teaching of **JESUS**.

All written directly from live happenings because they hand over hands-on experience walking life with **JESUS** under the **HOLY SPIRIT'S** instructions.

The **fourth part** is to learn who **JESUS** was and to know **HIM** in all **HIS** glory. The word **JESUS** is repeated 973 times in the **BIBLE**. **JESUS** is out of **GOD**. Everything that exists or existed is out of **GOD**. Sometimes the question gets asked: Why did **GOD** create **JESUS**? But whatever we say about **JESUS** I just say with **GODLY** respect, **JESUS** was there from the beginning. In **GOD'S WORD** it says **JESUS** was there from the start. So for now let's say **JESUS** had three tasks that **HE** fulfills:

Firstly to go to earth in flesh to teach us of the **GODHEAD**, **secondly** to die for all our sins on the cross and overpower the devil by taken the keys of hell. And **thirdly** to sit on **HIS** throne to judge the believer of his works by fire. Good lets introduce you to **JESUS**.

About 2000 years ago a child was born in Bethlehem. Whilst we have read in the **OLD TESTAMENT** a number of times that a savior will be born on earth.

In Ps 17:7 David speaks to **GOD** "*Show Your marvelous loving kindness by Your right hand, O You who save those who trust in You from those who rise up against them.*"

Tit 3:4 "*But when the kindness and the love of God our Savior toward man appeared,*"

Isa 59:20 "*The Redeemer will come to Zion, and to those who turn from transgression in Jacob, says the LORD.*"

Isa 9:6 "*For unto us a Child is born, unto us a Son is given; and the government will be upon His shoulder. And His name will be called Wonderful, Counselor, Mighty God, Everlasting Father, Prince of Peace.*"

Gal 4:4 "*But when the fullness of the time had come, God sent forth His Son, born of a woman, born under the law,*"

Rom 1:3 "*concerning His Son Jesus Christ our Lord, who was born of the seed of David according to the flesh,*"

Luk 2:11 "*For there is born to you this day in the city of David a Savior, who is Christ the Lord.*"

Now **JESUS** had to come out of **HIS SPIRITUAL** dimension to flesh and had to reveal **HIMSELF** as man to the human beings so that all human can believe that **HE** came, and see otherwise they would have said he is an angel if he would have come in spirit. **HE** had to be a baby first and walk on earth and had all human characters and that the world could see **HIM** and believe in **HIM**.

From 12 year old age JESUS starts to teach people out of GOD'S WORD the OLD TESTAMENT in the temple whilst HIS parents went to offer and pray in Jerusalem.

Now the power of GOD was in HIM and worked through HIM. We read in Luk 1:35 *"And the angel answered and said to her, " The Holy Spirit will come upon you, and the power of the Highest will overshadow you; therefore, also, that Holy One who is to be born will be called the Son of God."*

JESUS had the power of GOD in HIM. We read about many miracles JESUS did, healed people's bodies, the sick, and healed people of their sins, forgave people of their sins and even raised people out of death. JESUS had all power on earth as HE had in heaven. This brings us at the part of JESUS'S teaching. HE came to earth to teach us about GOD, and GOD'S SPIRIT and about the heavens and eternity.

Heb 5:8 *"though He was a Son, yet He learned obedience by the things which He suffered. And having been perfected, He became the author of eternal salvation to all who obey Him, called by God as High Priest "according to the order of Melchizedek,"* JESUS had to be obedient to HIS FATHER GOD.

We read in Joh 3:5 *"Jesus answered, "Most assuredly, I say to you, unless one is born of water and the Spirit, he cannot enter the kingdom of God."* As new born Christian, it is a step of obedience and gets to wash his sins away by following JESUS through baptism in water. Isn't it true that JESUS was baptised by John the Baptist in the Jordan River? Also in 1Pet 1:23 *"having been born again, not of corruptible seed but incorruptible, through the word of God which lives and abides forever,"* There is also a module written of "Who is JESUS" which you can request. So JESUS lives on the earth between people, teaches people, and does all miracles before people.

Many believed in **HIM** and accepted **GOD** and then there was many under the law like the Pharisees and Sadducees who was suppose to be the representatives of the olden church and knew the **WORD** of **GOD** but didn't believe in the coming of **JESUS**.

Later through **JESUS'S** teaching they were the tempters from the devil who kept on hustling **JESUS** in all that he taught the people. John the Baptist was the forerunner for **JESUS** and told everybody that there is a savior coming. He baptised people in the name of the **FATHER, SON** and **HOLY SPIRIT**. Tempted by the Pharisees and saw that there were many of them whilst he was doing his called job he said: Mat 3:7 *"But when he saw many of the Pharisees and Sadducees coming to his baptism, he said to them, "Brood of vipers! Who warned you to flee from the wrath to come?"*. The **BIBLE** says that **JESUS** was Baptised by John in Mat 3:16 *"When He had been baptized, Jesus came up immediately from the water; and behold, the heavens were opened to Him, and He saw the Spirit of God descending like a dove and alighting upon Him."* **JESUS** had to be obedient to **GOD** and always said: *"And suddenly a voice came from heaven, saying, this is My beloved Son, in whom I am well pleased."* This was where **GOD** admitted to the world that **JESUS** is his sent **SON**, who follows **HIS** demand and does all the necessary steps to follow **GOD**. Therefore the baptism through water bath shows us a sign that **HE** also follows **HIS FATHER'S** command and being obedient. Also to us a sign of obedience that we accept **HIM** purifies us from our sins through the water bath of faith.

It's a sign from our side that we accept **HIM** and follow **HIM** alone. I have also written a module on Baptism which you can request and study. The BIBLE says in Eph 4:5 *"one Lord, one faith, one baptism;"* and we as human beings does not need to argue about the method of Baptism, but just do it as a step of faith to follow **JESUS** also through the baptism bath.

We are now set to look at the crucifixion of **JESUS** the one reason why **HE** had to come to earth, and a bit later we talk about the happenings around **HIS** death. To be obedient to **HIS FATHER**, **JESUS** had to die on the cross and **HIS BLOOD** had to flow from the cross for all human beings and with **HIS** suffering bought freedom for us from sin. Remember when you pray your repentance prayer: we accept **HIM** as our savior and profess our **CHRIST** religion and forgiveness of our sins **HE** already took away through **HIS** death on the cross. What does it mean when we say: **JESUS** is the **MEDIATOR**? Read in 1Tim 2:5 *"For there is one God and one Mediator between God and men, the Man Christ Jesus,"* and then we also read in Heb 9:15 *"And for this reason He is the Mediator of the new covenant, by means of death, for the redemption of the transgressions under the first covenant, that those who are called may receive the promise* *of the eternal inheritance."* When we pray **JESUS** is the **MEDIATOR** between us and **GOD**. As example we pray to **GOD** and we ask things in **JESUS'S NAME**.

In the next chapters we deal in depth with the last reason why **JESUS** had to come to earth and that is: He had to go and sit in **HIS** judgment chair in heaven awaiting the period to judge the believers works with fire to see if your works on earth will withstand. Read 2 Cor 5:10 *"For we must all appear before the judgment seat of Christ, that each one may receive the things done in the body, according to what he has done, whether good or bad."* Nobody who lived on earth will escape the two judgments in heaven. The unbeliever will not be at the same heavenly ceremony than the believer, but will appear in front of the white throne judgment where **GOD HIMSELF** will judge them and cast them into hell. You will read all about that in the following chapters.

This brings us to the **fifth section** and the most important and most difficult part to write about and that is **GOD** the **HEAVENLY FATHER** you need to know and meet. **GOD** is love.

Before I attempt to write anything about **GOD** I say this with the greatest respect and humbleness. Without **GOD** nothing happened in the past, and nothing now, and nothing in the future. There are not enough words or neither paper on earth to describe our **GOD ALMIGHTY**. **HIS** greatness, **HIS** goodness and **HIS** wonder. **HIS WORD** describes **HIM** the best, let's read in Gen 1:1 *"In the beginning God created the heavens and the earth. The earth was without form, and void; and darkness* was on the face of the deep. And the Spirit of God was hovering over the face of the waters." So **GOD** is spirit. Now if earth and the heavens are not fantastic which we are part of what is? Heavens at night is like a massive drawing board when you look up. **HE** is larger than the biggest imaginative picture you can imagine. Overwhelmed with the next thing **GOD** does? Verse 3 *"Then God said, "Let there be light"; and there was light. "* Think about it, who on earth can say let there be light and it happens. NO! NOBODY! And all of a sudden the sun rotates around his axis. Just think what happened that instant!

Have you studied or read about what the scientists said and think they know about the sun, I think **GOD** thinks let them dream on. Nobody could get close enough to the sun to know exactly what it consists off. If you take a couple of minutes and look at a video clip of "Louie Giglio – Indescribable and also How Great is **GOD**". He said imagine the day light, the sun happened you wouldn't have liked to be close to what happened when **GOD** opened his mouth and said: "Let there be light" The sun is flying out at the speed of light at about 186 000 miles/second into the sky. What a powerful light flash that would have been, you cannot imagine that.

Have you ever tried to look up into the sun with bare eyes? Also looked at lightning in a rainstorm close to you? And at night time how powerful and intense the white bright light stream is like to bear with your eyes.

That is only a fraction of what happened when **GOD** said let there be light and with one boom it all happened. Have you stood in front of a massive mountain and looked up? You are getting the feeling you are so small.

But our **LIVING GOD** is still meddling with us and we still think our biggest problem on earth is big! Our **GOD** is indescribably big and hence the reason I dare not try to describe **GOD** in my plainness and humbleness. **HE** is massive and also our **MAJESTY**. With the size of us versus **GOD** he still comes in **HIS WORD** and says: *"I am here to make a dwelling in you"* and that gives us the guarantee that **GOD** made us and long before birth he knew our name and wants to be our **FATHER** and wants you to serve **HIM**.

This brings us at the **sixth section** and the **third part** of the **GODHEAD** the **HOLY SPIRIT** of **GOD**. The word **HOLY SPIRIT** is written 1079 times in the **BIBLE**. The **HOLY SPIRIT** is **GOD'S SPIRIT**. There are no barriers for **GOD'S SPIRIT**. The **BIBLE** describes **HIM** as omnipresent. The **HOLY SPIRIT** testifies to us of **GOD'S** existence. We read in Heb 10:15 *"But the Holy Spirit also witnesses to us; for after He had said before,"* Remember when John the Baptist said in Mar 1:8 *"I indeed baptized you with water, but He"* this is now **JESUS** *"will baptize you with the Holy Spirit."* At this point I just need to mention to you the importance of this, when a newly born Christian gives his live and heart to **GOD** the **HOLY SPIRITS** voice begins to be actively present in you. From that moment you need to have a new clean lifestyle and try your ultimate to stay like that. A question that pops up is why doesn't the **HOLY SPIRIT** stop me to sin? Precisely **GOD** gives you the choice and opens the communication channel in your mind to speak to **HIM** to talk to **HIM** through his **SPIRIT** and then when you pray you pray through **JESUS** the only **MEDIATOR** to **GOD**.

Look at Luk 12:12 *"For the Holy Spirit will teach you in that very hour what you ought to say."* **GOD'S SPIRIT** wants to speak to you and support you to have and lead a clean life as **GOD** intended you to be from your existence. Think about it, **GOD** gives you the freedom to choose what you want to say or do when evil come your way.

The **BIBLE** refers to many times in the olden days how the **HOLY SPIRIT** came upon people and is still the same today. Read in Act 13:52 *"And the disciples were filled with joy and with the Holy Spirit."* Then we read in 2 Tim 1:14 *"That good thing which was committed to you, keep by the Holy Spirit who dwells in us."*

Many people belief that the **HOLY SPIRIT** didn't occur in the Old Testament times, but it did, let us look at Ps 51:13 *"Do not cast me away from Your presence, and do not take Your Holy Spirit from me."* The **HOLY SPIRIT** brings **GOD'S** message to the human being and sometimes without us knowing it, we listen to a sermon in your church and then after you speak to a friend or family member in another country, the same message was given by **GOD'S SPIRIT** to all. Isn't it fantastic and **GODLY** to know that the same message was giving to various preachers? So we all get the same message. **GOD** says: *"I am yesterday, today and forever the same."* We are also sealed until the day when we get relieved from this world. Read in Eph 4: 30 *"And do* *not grieve the Holy Spirit of God, by whom you were sealed for the day of redemption."*

Now whilst we talk about that it is important to know that the only unforgiving sin is to sin against the **HOLY SPIRIT**. Read Mar 3:29 *"but he who blasphemes against the Holy Spirit never has forgiveness, but is subject to eternal condemnation"* we know the word blasphemes means to speak untrue things, and by purpose harm somebody's character, without have real evidence. **JESUS** was also guided by the **HOLY SPIRIT** whilst he was on earth. We read in Luk4:1 *"Then Jesus, being filled with the Holy Spirit, returned from the Jordan and was led by the Spirit into the wilderness,"* and we know this part where **JESUS** was tempted by the devil in the desert. Also need to add the **HOLY SPIRIT** gave **JESUS** assistance against the evil temptations. We can get so much more and ask **GOD** more knowing that **JESUS** died on the cross to give us fullness in **GOD** with the **HOLY SPIRIT** living in us.

Many more references in the **BIBLE**, but can't write all down now where the **HOLY SPIRIT** gives us guidance, and **GODLY** insight assisting us on our path. Also many references where the **HOLY SPIRIT** came upon many people, where they speak in tongues and foreign languages. Paul said remember all have different gifts. The **HOLY SPIRIT** came unto flesh on Whit Sunday like a fire out of heaven. In Act 2:4 *"And they were all filled with the Holy Spirit and began to speak with other tongues, as the Spirit gave them utterance."*

When you study in **GOD'S WORD** the **Holy SPIRIT** comes to teach you and open scripture to you and help you to understand. Sometimes you read a verse and get no understanding, but when you pray and ask the **HOLY SPIRIT** to open it for you, then you instantly see things. Remember it is not only when you are sad or in need that you can talk to the **HOLY SPIRIT** but the more you talk to **HIM** the easier your life become. Our time gets robbed by evil things, so you need to be constantly talking to the **HOLY SPIRIT** and to prevent evil destructions. For the closure I just want to say you need to be careful how your time is getting robbed by rubbish. You only get saved ones and maybe think that no sin can get to you and that you won't get tempted again. It will absolutely be now that the evil will put hurdles for you to fall again to go back to the broad road that leads to hell. Read in Heb 6:4 to 6 *"For it is impossible for those who were once enlightened, and have tasted the heavenly gift, and have become partakers of the Holy Spirit, 5 and have tasted the good word of God and the powers of the age to come, 6 if they fall away, to renew them again to repentance, since they crucify again for themselves the Son of God, and put Him to an open shame."*

The **seventh part** your church. Where do you work for **GOD**? To witch church do you belong? Which church is correct for me? The main question is not which church, domination or believe is right for me. The **WORD** of **GOD** is your guideline in that. You can't after you belong to a congregation come and go as you please. If you feel the leaders of the congregation is not within the **BIBLE** then it is your choice to stay and talk to the leaders after you prayed about it. It is not your decision to change the church or leaders.

GOD is in control of **HIS** church and normally the fault lies with us human beings. Remember your work in the church never ends.

Paul wrote letters to all congregations and sometimes had to warn them about their sins and wrong doings with brothers and sister. You too can get your insight like Paul to assist people in church with the always lead of the **HOLY SPIRIT**. Let us read 1Cor 6:19 *"Or do you not know that your body is the temple of the Holy Spirit who is in you, whom you have from God, and you are not your own?"* Just like we are in a church as a congregation we are the body of **CHRIST**.

The **eighth part**, your **work in GOD'S body**. You as one member of the body need to concentrate to work hard to bring people closer to **GOD** and not try to boost yourself. Now you realise why it is important to grow in **GOD'S** work in a church under the **SPIRIT** and **HIS** people. Remember **GOD** is the head of the congregation and if leaders are not qualified to work according to the **SPIRIT** of **GOD**, **HE** will remove them on **HIS** own time and on **HIS** manner. Don't labour under false condition to try and gain humanly, you belong to **GOD** and he is your **FATHER**, **HE** is the **HEAD**, **HE** is the one that everybody in the congregation praise and worship in truth. Remember **HE** could move you out as well, it is important to be pure as a whole in the congregation inside and outside, we are living for **GOD** not for men. **JESUS** said: Luk 9:23 *"Then He said to them all,"If anyone desires to come after Me, let him deny himself, and take up his cross daily, and follow Me."*

JESUS said: *"For what profit is it to a man if he gains the whole world, and is himself destroyed or lost?"* Also read Luk 9:25 *"For what profit is it to a man if he gains the whole world, and is himself destroyed or lost?"* We are running this race to earn eternity at **JESUS** and **GOD**. If you are called to play music, to be a deacon, an elder, it does not matter how simple the task in **GOD'S** house is do it with all your strength and not for self gain. But only to reconcile with **GOD** and the expansion of **HIS KINGDOM** and **GLORY**.

It brings us to the **ninth part, healing**. This is one of the major stumble blocks of the believers. Not only healing of the body, spiritual, spiritual constraint and crippled. I have also written a module about healing which you can request. We first look at body healing.

The **BIBLE** is full of healing and miracles not only done by **JESUS** when **HE** was on earth, but **GOD** used ordinary human beings to perform such a talent with great success. Even the disciples performed healing. In today's life we hear of many testimonies where people prayed for healing and there were full healing and recovery. We praise **GOD** for people who listen to **GOD** and keep on working under the sick. This takes us to faith; many people get **HIS** healing to believe in healing.

Remember the old saying of the mustard seed? It happens most of the time with the believer, or should I say the children of **GOD**, but not only them even with the unbeliever where the believer prays and they get instant healing by the favour of **GOD** working through the believer to show the world of unbelief that **HE** is in control. So the question pops up, why only the believers? Because of your belief in the **GODHEAD** and you believe in the working of the **SPIRIT**, because belief is **SPIRITUAL** and the unbeliever must be exalted to see the power of **GOD** before believing. Most of the healing of **JESUS** when **HE** was on earth **HE** said unto them: Your faith or your sins are forgiven and then they healed instantly. And remember on top of all, we are all created by **GOD** and **HE** is the only creator of life.

Healing goes hand to hand with sin. Read Mat 9:6 *"But that you may know that the Son of Man has power on earth to forgive sins"—then He said to the paralytic,"Arise, take up your bed, and go to your house."* The same for spiritual sickness, spiritual constraint. In today's life it became so easy to fall under the word "stress" , everybody make excuses for sins committed and all take the stress escape or side track away from the principles **GOD** has put in place. NO definitely NOT, the **BIBLE** is full of miracles from **GOD** and was definitely not stress, but perfect work through **HIM**.

GOD is perfect and we belong to **HIM** and we see his work is perfect. Don't fall under mislead of the evil which can be broken with fasting and prayer to the only living **GOD**. What happened when **JESUS** chased the evil spirits into the pigs? We read that in Mat 8:30. Read what **JESUS** said in Mat 12:39 to 45 " 45 *"Then he goes and takes with him seven other spirits more wicked than himself, and they enter and dwell there; and the last state of that man is worse than the first. So shall it also be with this wicked generation."* People please look at these sections, there is many in the **BIBLE** you need to look at, and see it is the evil driven from the hell.

Read Luk 7:2, Eph 6:12, Act 19:12 & 13 and Mat 12:45 the works of **JESUS** and **HIS** image speaks of **GODLY** power and all healing are possible through faith only. Not through evil works and not through artificial deceit. **JESUS** also healed brokenness, lamed men and also the dead. David talks in Psalms about healing Ps 41:5 *"I said, "LORD, be merciful to me; heal my soul, for I have sinned against You."* Read the complete Psalm. Also read Mar 3:14 *"Then He appointed twelve, that they might be with Him and that He might send them out to preach,*15 *"and to have power to heal sicknesses and to cast out demons:"* We as believers have the power and authority to heal people through prayer and they who believe will receive healing in **JESUS** name.

The next is the **tenth section, blessing** and **sighing**. (Moaning) Many people struggle to think what they could do to get blessed. We as children of **GOD** are privilege because we are blessed just to be a child of **GOD**. The privilege we have to be a reborn Christian is a blessing and the best thing that can happen to you whilst you are on earth. There is nothing earthly greater than this: your name is written in the **BOOK** of **LIFE**, what a blessing. Now you start sharing your blessings with others. Firstly with your household, then your family, your neighbours and your congregation members, your brothers and sisters in **CHRIST**.

JESUS said: *"Long before you pray your FATHER in heaven knows what you need"* The greatest conformation in **GOD'S WORD** is in Mat 6:33 & 34 *"But seek first the kingdom of God and His righteousness, and all these things shall be added to you. 34 Therefore do not worry about tomorrow, for tomorrow will worry about its own things. Sufficient for the day is its own trouble."*

When we work in the field of soul saving, we pray for souls given to us to lead and convert to **JESUS**. If a soul has repent the angles in heaven celebrates for one returned to **GOD**. When that happens it is a blessing and not only on earth, but in heaven when you have to receive a crown from **JESUS** the judgment day when your works will be tested by fire. **GOD** bless you with prosperity, in our work, our financials, your marriage and partnership, your happiness, your house, your vehicle, your clothes and food just to mention a few blessings.

Remember when **JESUS** said in the Beatitudes in Mat 5, 6 and 7, it was clearly said by **HIM** that **GOD** is our provider of all our needs. We just need to remember to contribute to **HIS** house, for **HIS** work, other institutions that assist the needy, just a bit of your prosperity. The **BIBLE** also says: Bring a tenth of your income to **MY** house so that we feast in abundance. Also **GOD** said: test me in this to receive a blessing with all you need. Read in 1Chron 29:17 *"I know also, my God, that You test the heart and have pleasure in uprightness. As for me, in the uprightness of my heart I have willingly offered all these things; and now with joy I have seen Your people, who are present here to offer willingly to You."* When you give, **GOD** gives back by multitude. You may also divide blessings to the needed and receive blessings through that. Read again in Mat 5:44 *"But I say to you, love your enemies, bless those who curse you,"* and understand **GOD** gives to the believers and unbelievers. When you receive all from **GOD** and **HIS LOVE** you realise how blessed you are to be a child of **GOD**. When we give, we give with an open heart, even if it is not a lot, we read in the **WORD** about the woman who threw her last in the treasure chest in front of **JESUS** in Mar 12:41 to 44 *"42 "Then one poor widow came and threw in two mites, which make a quadrant. 43 So He called His disciples to Himself and said to them, "Assuredly, I say to you that this poor widow has put in more than all those who have given to the treasury;"*

When we look at Job he was a rich man and said: Job 23:10 *"But He knows the way that I take; when He has tested me, I shall come forth as gold."*

Remember we will go through this in the coming chapters, where we will be tested by fire on the believer's judgment? Then we look at what the **BIBLE** said about sighing or moaning of the child of **GOD**, when we know we are human as well, despondent and sighing. In Prov 29:2 *"When the righteous are in authority, the people rejoice; But when a wicked man rules, the people groan."* We read that even JESUS sighs in Mar 7:34 *"Then, looking up to heaven, He sighed, and said to him, "Ephphatha,"that is, "Be opened."* We know that the whole creation sigh and together in travail up to now waiting for JESUS to come. So the question what should I do as reborn child of GOD? Look what was said in Rom 8:26 *"Likewise the Spirit also helps in our weaknesses. For we do not know what we should pray for as we ought, but the Spirit Himself makes intercession for us with groanings which cannot be uttered. 27 Now He who searches the hearts knows what the mind of the Spirit is, because He makes intercession for the saints according to the will of God."* Just think how much the non believer misses.

This brings us to the **eleventh part, spiritual war fare.** We know the **BIBLE** is very specific in telling us who we fight against. Lets read in Eph 6:12 *"For we do not wrestle against flesh and blood, but against principalities, against powers, against the rulers of the darkness of this age, against spiritual hosts of wickedness in the heavenly places."* You and I know that from the start the devil let us fall under sin and tempted all on earth. The **BIBLE** is full of scriptures about the evil works and it is written that the devil has always been a deceiver and liar with his works.

But that brought us to the point where we accepted **GOD**. That moment we gave ourselves over to **HIM**, that was when **GOD** took control of our lives.

As we discovered in the previous section and walking a religious path with **GOD**, are there are many things we have discovered about the **GODHEAD** and ultimate power is our source the **HOLY SPIRIT** in our heart, life and took control of our body. We tap into the power of the **HOLY SPIRIT**, through **JESUS** to **GOD**. *"**GOD** says whatever you ask in **HIS NAME** thy will receive."* It works for us now to praise **GOD** in truth and never stop praying.

As reborn baby in **CHRIST** you start to learn from scratch to disregard all the old wrong doings, and or wrong saying to others in the past and have to let go immediately. From day one you start to grow. In 1 Cor 13:11 *"When I was a child, I spoke as a child, I understood as a child, I thought as a child; but when I became a man, I put away childish things."* May **GOD'S SPIRIT** teach you to grow to maturity in **HIS** work? May I remind you again about the eternal price, a crown from **JESUS**; because our name is written in the book of life and we will be with **JESUS** and **GOD**.

Brings us at the **twelfth section, eternal life**. As introduction I need to tell you as a new Christian that there are no non believers, sinners, and liars and people who doesn't want to accept **GOD** as their personal savior in heaven and with eternal life. The reason **JESUS** said to his disciples to not keep the children away from him. Mat 19:14 *"But Jesus said, "Let the little children come to Me, and do not forbid them; for of such is the kingdom of heaven."* The first very important fact I need to mention before we touch children of eternal life is the word abortion and never named in the **BIBLE** and created by human driven from the liar out of the realm of death. In some countries abortion is legal and in other countries it is law and punishable as a criminal act. What the human being became is not what **JESUS** and **GOD** planned and described in the **BIBLE**.

You cannot take a life after **GOD** has given them life." *and do not forbid them; for of such is the kingdom of heaven."* What is the true meaning when **GOD** said you will leave your mother and father and be one with your wife or husband? The natural and **GODLY** cause is seeds planted by you and **GOD** will give life. After **GOD** has given life you as a human being have no authority to take life. Why do you think a miscarriage comes naturally? **GOD** is the only one controlling life. In Western Australia alone 14 babies are getting killed a day and could have been spiritual bodies working for **GOD** and to praise and give **GOD** glory. A newborn child is pure and without sin. Now the question why are they not born with sin? Definitely not, listen to what **JESUS** said: *"If you were like a child you would have inherited eternal life"* The adult's image is a reflection on their children.

Think about it; the small pure child changed by the parents. That's why **JESUS** said: Bring those children to me. The **WORD** says: *"Jesus laid his hands on them and blessed them"* Why do you think he did that?

The children can't guard themselves against life. Let's look at the following: Mat 18:1 to 14 *"At that time the disciples came to*

Jesus, saying, "Who then is greatest in the kingdom of heaven? 2 Then Jesus called a little child to Him, set him in the midst of them, 3 and said, "Assuredly, I say to you, unless you are converted and become as little children, you will by no means enter the kingdom of heaven. 4 Therefore whoever humbles himself as this little child is the greatest in the kingdom of heaven." And now the following is one massive tip **JESUS** gave us to achieve and get to the crown of **GOD** in verse 5 " *Whoever receives one little child like this in My name receives Me."*

Parents be careful how you bring your children up! Is it for the **Kingdom** of **GOD** or do you risk losing eternal life. Then in the following verse 10 **JESUS** gives that to our benefit as parents:

"Take heed that you do not despise one of these little ones, for I say to you that in heaven their angels always see the face of My Father who is in heaven." Read the full chapter for your own benefit and may I suggest you keep your **BIBLE** close by for the rest of the book where I give you guidelines and please make notes or highlight the important verses to assist you with your growing journey in **CHRIST**.

Please pray with me:

Father we praise YOU and give YOU all honor and ask YOU to wake our spirit up to learn through YOUR SPIRIT of truth and open our hearts to accept and receive YOUR WORD which we know are YOU like you said in John 1 verse 1 : In the beginning was the WORD, and the WORD was with GOD, and the WORD was GOD. HOLY SPIRIT holds our attention on the truth of your WORD and not gets confused until JESUS come to fetch us. We pray this in JESUS name.

AMEN

Live after Death

BIBLE references:

Rom 8:10-39	Gal 5:25	Rom 12:2	Gal 2:20	Joh 1:1-4
1 Pet 1:23 & 25	Joh 8:11	Gen 4:7	Mat 6:9-13	Mat 5,6 & 7
Mat 6:9	1 Cor 16:29	Jon 4:4	Mat 18: 18 & 19	Mat 10:31
Ps 119:11	Joh 8:7	Luk 17:6	Mat 17:20	Jam 1:6
Jon 1:12	Rom 8:14	Rom 9:8	Col 3:16	Mat 5:9
Rom 8:16	Jon 5:2	1 Joh 3:10	Rom 8:21	Ps 17:7
Tit 3:4	Isa 59:20	Isa 9:5	Gal 4:4	Rom 1:3
Luk 2:11	Luk 1:35	Joh 3:5	1Pet 1:23	Mat 3:7&11
Mat 3:16&17	Eph 4:5	1Tim 2:5	1Tim 2:5	2 Cor 5:10
Gen 1:1 to 3	Heb 10:15	Mar 1:8	Luk 12:12	Act 13:52
2 Tim 1:14	Ps 51:13	Eph 4: 30	Mar 3:29	Luk 4:1
Act 2:4	Heb 6:4 to 6	1Cor 6:19	Luk 9:23	Luk 9:25
Mat 3:17	Mat 8:30	Mat 12:39 to 45	Luk 7:2	Eph 6:12
Act 19:12&13	Mat 12:45	Ps 41:5	Mar 3:14	Mat 6:33 & 34
Cron 29:17	Mat 5:44	Mar 12:41 to 44	Job 23:10	Prov 29:2
Mar 7:34	Rom 8:26	Eph 6:12	1 Cor 13:11	Mat 19:14
Mat 18:1 to 14				

How should I start? | 41

Notes:

Chapter 2
Five minutes after death of a believer

We read in Luk 16:19-31 a story **JESUS** *told to explain the things after death. Some say it really happened and some believe it was a true story. Now the man died and wasn't dead. This is a well known parable in Luke 16 about the rich man and Lazarus. Do you know it?* **JESUS** *gave this to bring a bit of light to the unknown. And it took place in the after death with a conversation between the two dead. Take it as a true story for the ease of mind, and then later you will see references to today's life as well. The* **BIBLE** *says from verse: 19 "There was a certain rich man who was clothed in purple and fine linen and fared sumptuously every day. 20 But there was a certain beggar named Lazarus, full of sores, who was laid at his gate, 21 desiring to be fed with the crumbs which fell from the rich man's table. Moreover the dogs came and licked his sores. 22 So it was that the beggar died, and was carried by the angels to Abraham's bosom. The rich man also died and was buried. 23 And being in torments in Hades, he lifted up his eyes and saw Abraham* *afar off, and Lazarus in his bosom. 24 Then he cried and said, 'Father Abraham, have mercy on me, and send Lazarus that he may dip the tip of his finger in water and cool my tongue; for I am tormented in this flame.' 25 But Abraham said, 'Son, remember that in your lifetime you received your good things, and likewise Lazarus evil things; but now he is comforted and you are tormented. 26 And besides all this, between us and you there is a great gulf fixed, so that those who want to pass from here to you cannot, nor can those from there pass to us.' 27 Then he said, 'I beg you therefore, father, that you would send him to my father's house, 28 for I have five brothers, that he may testify to them, lest they also come to this place of torment.' 29 Abraham said to him, 'They have Moses and the prophets; let them hear them.' 30 And he said, 'No, father Abraham; but if one goes to them from the dead, they will repent.'*

31 But he said to him, 'If they do not hear Moses and the prophets, neither will they be persuaded though one rise from the dead.' "

Strangely **JESUS** only mentions the name of Lazarus and not the rich man as in verse 20. Lazarus was assured a child of **GOD**. This subject is in context of the believer and life after death. And in the next chapter "Life after death of a non believer." At this point I declare that the **BIBLE** is the only book giving you good information of the life after death. Now the question: Will you see your own death personally as a blessing or a judgement? Have you ever wondered what the death is and what awaits you after death? What happens to a child of **GOD** when a believer departs this life? All answers like this and about that are in the **BIBLE**. We are definitely going to look at that now. What is death? The **BIBLE** is clear on that in Jam 2:26 *"For as the body without the spirit is dead, so faith without works is dead also."* That's what death is, death starts immediately after your spirit leaves your body. Most of the heart surgeons are saying: clinical death is when your heart stops and you are not breathing anymore, while biological death starts when all tissue died, and there are no function happening in your body. For this reason we say death comes about 4 to 6 minutes after your heart stopped.

Also true what King Salomon said in Acc 12:7 *"Then the dust will return to the earth as it was, and the spirit will return to God who gave it."* Adam was formed from dust of the earth, when you depart this life your spirit goes back to **GOD**, because **HE** gave you your spirit.

See what Gen 2:7 says: *"And the Lord God formed man of the dust of the ground, and breathed into his nostrils the breath of life; and man became a living being."* Just like that the human being became a living soul, a living spirit. Interesting when we look at an explanation of the new dictionary word, that the separation of the soul of the spiritual soul of man from the body, material part the lattice seizing part and turning to dust.

Both the people in Luk 16 the rich man and Lazarus proposed by **JESUS** went somewhere directly after they departed from life into another dimension or state or spiritual life. Isn't that what it says: when the rich man died immediately he finds himself in hell, and when he looks up! As if he was not dead he looks up.

Same with Lazarus. When he died in Luk 16:22 he was curried by angels to father Abraham's bosom. And I think that is happening with you when you are a child of **GOD**. So when you die **GOD'S** angels take you to **HIM** and got to be your guardian angel as well. When you die your body is dead and your spirit departs to another place. It is very interesting to study in **GOD'S** word to see what **HE** says about the believer when he or she departs from life.

There are other death scenarios you can read about in the **BIBLE**, but we are looking at Lazarus when **JESUS** told this story. The name Lazarus in Hebrew means "Elieser" and in Greek it means "**GOD** is my rescue". Here we have a beggar and he is rescued by **GOD** and while he was alive his name did not mean anything, he was sitting begging outside the rich man's house. This could be a great lesson to us here. We shouldn't evaluate people on their looks or what they have in life, nor their position in life. Maybe a good thing is to evaluate people by their faith, their good deeds and maybe their relationship with the living **GOD** and **HIS SON JESUS CHRIST**.

In verse 22 we read the moment the beggar died he was carried by angels to the bosom of Abraham. Very informative of **JESUS** and it is by implication that he says the believer is taken by angles the moment they die to the new place where they continue to exist. Take note of this. I will take you back to Mat 18:2 and specifically verse 10 " ***Take heed that you do not*** *despise one of these little ones, for I say to you that in heaven their angels always see the face of My Father who is in heaven."* So that the angles know what happen to children and **GOD** sees what happens. It is very important that angels know when a baby is born. Angels are also aware when a sinner repents.

In Luk 15:10 **JESUS** said: *"Likewise, I say to you, there is joy in the presence of the angels of God over one sinner who repents."* The angels of **GOD** know on earth when somebody repents and the message is taken to heaven. The angels re joys when one sinner repents.

Angels know when you repent as sinner, they are aware of it, and takes you when you depart from life to eternity, to their paradise.

When we read in 2 Cor 12:2 to 4 about heavens, paradise is in the third heaven. Here **JESUS** says in Mat 16:22 the beggar dies and was carried by angles. They were his companion. They took him to the bosom of Abraham. So after life is not the end. This is what **GOD** provided for us as believers, eternal life after death. So **HE** says Lazarus was at father Abrahams bosom and fully aware of Abraham. By the way when you read in Mat 17:4 *"Then Peter answered and said to Jesus, Lord, it is good for us to be here; if You wish, let us make here three tabernacles: one for You, one for Moses, and one for Elijah"* Peter, James and John saw Moses and Elijah, and could recognise them without **JESUS** telling them.

This was on the mount of worship when **JESUS** was glorified by **GOD**, **HE** changed and has this bright light around **HIM** and there were two others with **JESUS**, then the disciples said to **JESUS** can we build a hut for **YOU**, Moses and Elijah. So they recognise them. The believers get comfort, attend to and protected after death. We read in verse 23 *and Lazarus was at the bosom of Abraham*. In verse 25 *Abraham spoke about Lazarus and said to the rich man, remember that in your lifetime you received your good things, and likewise Lazarus evil things, but now he is comforted and you are tormented.* The believer is on the place where he was comforted, attended to and protected, forever away, separated from the non believer. When the rich man asked Abraham if Lazarus could bring him a drop of water, Abraham said: *And besides all this, between us and you there is a great gulf fixed.* This is definitely an unbridgeable time in life after death. Hereafter when you die without **GOD** there is no second opportunity, you will be lost forever.

Heb 9:27 is clear *"And as it is appointed for men to die once, but after this the judgment."*

The question arises why are all believers going to heaven? The answer is simple, because the believer's name is written in the book of life. In Luk 10:20 the disciples came back happy that the demons submit to them **JESUS** said: *"Nevertheless do not rejoice in this, that the spirits are subject to you, but rather rejoice because your names are written in heaven. "*

That was a humanly achievement and they thought that was good, but that was not the most important thing. When your name is written in the book of life then you will joyfully go to eternity. The devils submit them to **JESUS** and flee away from him. It is exactly what Paul says: Phil 4:4 *"Rejoice in the Lord always. Again I will say, rejoice!"* And whoever's name is written like Lazarus's name in the book of life and called the day of judgement will be in heaven, but non believers like the rich man's name was never mentioned in the book of life. If you die without **GOD** you are nameless, but if you die in **CHRIST** you will be receiving a new name as promised in Revelation *"HE gives you a new name"* Have you wondered why the rich man didn't have a name? When you die as a non believer you are nothing, because you are in a pool of fire, first in the realm of death, and then in the hell forever. Question what does it look like on the other side of death? I want to share this with you.

In Heb 12:22 *"But you have come to Mount Zion and to the city of the living God, the heavenly Jerusalem, to an innumerable company of angels, 23 to the general assembly and church of the firstborn who are registered in heaven, to God the Judge of all, to the spirits of just men made perfect, 24 to Jesus the Mediator of the new covenant, and to the blood of sprinkling that speaks better things than that of Abel."* Let us look at this lovely comfort; because Abraham says to the rich man Lazarus is getting comforted. Now how does the lovely comfort look like hereafter? In a couple of minutes the believer finds himself in the splendour of **GOD**.

Here we find it written what's waiting for the believer. Firstly there is a heavenly greeting, this place is called heaven. The city of the living **GOD**. **GOD** is not a **GOD** of the dead. **HE** is a living

GOD. The **GOD** of Abraham, Isaac and Jacob is still alive today. The only Living **GOD**.

You greeted the earthly, your town and surroundings and as child of **GOD** you are not earthely anymore. In the heaven city with the living **GOD** and as we know this city is located in heavens. In verse 22 we read this city is called the heavenly Jerusalem. The believer has citizenship of this city.

You are a citizen of heaven. And that is exactly what's written in Phil 3:20 *"For our citizenship is in heaven, from which we also eagerly wait for the Savior, the Lord Jesus Christ,"* You have a passport and in that passport its written that you are a citizen of your country, but in heaven we have a book as well, the book of live and your name will be in it. As a child of **GOD** your name is written in that book, and give you the right to access that city and you are a citizen through **JESUS CHRIST** which gives you access and it is limited to the believer. Not all people are going to that city, the opposite is people who are not allowed into the city and are much more than who is in the city. Let's see what **JESUS** said when the disciples asked him are the believer many or less? Rev 21:27 *"But there shall by no means enter it anything that defiles, or causes an abomination or a lie, but only those who are written in the Lamb's Book of Life."* Entrance is limited and without your name in the book of live, you will not have permission to enter the city. With that said we read in Heb 12:22 *"But you have come to Mount Zion and to the city of the living God, the heavenly Jerusalem, to an innumerable company of angels,"* There will be ten thousand times ten thousands of angles in heaven, and all the believers are all there. Even **GOD'S** angles are there and the **LAMB** will be there, the four living creatures will be there, the seraphines will be there, the Cherubims will be there, the twenty four elders. There will be ten thousands of ten thousands there. Read about that in Rev 5:7 to 14.

You will see and meet **GOD'S** angels, so you are going to a heavenly meeting, the moment you inherit heavens, when you blow out your last breath as child of **GOD** on earth, you go to this heavenly meeting. Secondly there is a heavenly gathering, the **BIBLE** calls it a festival meeting in verse 23 no sadness, no crying, but only festival. A national or global meeting where there will be a feast in the heavens. The conversion of one sinner has a huge impact on the angles in heaven. In Luk 15:10 *"Likewise, I say to you, there is joy in the presence of the angels of God over one sinner who repents."*

We believe there is a feast everyday in heaven, because many get saved on earth and they always have something to praise **GOD** for the new sinner that comes home.

Look in verse 23 who else is there the "Clusia" **GOD'S** church, the congregation, the firstborn of **JESUS CHRIST** whose names are written down.

There is definitely a clear thought of the book in heavens with names within. The **BIBLE** reconcile it in Rev 20 the saved of the congregation, the meeting of **GOD'S** children, HIS firstborn all of them is written into the book and we have the right to be glad that JESUS said to them you can start to be glad on earth that you have a name in heavens. **IS YOUR NAME THERE?** If you don't have anything else to be glad about, at least be glad that your name is in the book of live. With **GOD** the judge of all, in verse 23 and the **BIBLE** is not sentimental about it, **GOD** stays the judge of all. **HE** is the judge of the living and the dead. Over heaven and earth as well as over the realm of the dead. We all have to stand in front of the heavenly judge. With the spirits of all the truthful, there will be the believers. All **GOD'S** children's spirits, because their bodies are in earthly graves. Waiting for the resurrection 1Thess 4:14 to 18 explains what happens there and also 1 Cor 15:44 but I will discuss that a bit later in the book. Remember all the believers in heaven are perfect. It says at this side of the spirits of the truthful and when you die your sinful nature finishes and then all the believers in heaven are perfect.

No defects, no needs and listen what was written in Asa 25:8 *"He will swallow up death forever, and the Lord GOD will wipe away tears from all faces; the rebuke of His people He will take away from all the earth; For the LORD has spoken."* And also in Rev 7:17 and Rev 21: 4 *"And God will wipe away every tear from their eyes; there shall be no more death, nor sorrow, nor crying. There shall be no more pain, for the former things have passed away."* There will be no more dying.

No more sorrow, pain and difficulty, verse 5 says *"I renew everything"*. The spirits of all the saved people are there, the bodies in the graves and they all await the coming of **JESUS**, but their spirits are there. You are going to that meeting and there is a wonderful way to get there, and if you say I don't know how to get to heaven I can certainly say it is visible in the **BIBLE** and through **JESUS** through the blood of the New Testament.

Think about **JESUS** for a moment and if I ask you who do you want to see in heaven? David, Daniel, John or Paul, I would say none of the above I would like to see **JESUS** because if **JESUS** is there I know I am in heaven. **JESUS** said: I am the way, the truth and the life. **JESUS** is the **MEDIATOR** in Heb 12:24 **HE** is the **MEDIATOR** of the **NEW TESTAMENT** and **HE** mediated it through his blood on the cross, so **HE** is the only **MEDIATOR**. There is only one way to be saved in 1TIM 2:5 is definite and clear there is only one **GOD**, one **MEDIATOR**, and one **SAVIOR JESUS CHRIST**. The believer is an inheritance of heaven through the speaking of blood sprinkling better than Abel's blood. **GOD** said to Cain the blood of your brother calls for revenge Gen 4:10 *"And He said, "What have you done? The voice of your brother's blood cries out to Me from the ground."* **JESUS'S** blood calls for forgiveness and is an open way to **GOD**, **JESUS'S** blood opened the way to heavens so that you can now enter in the glory of **GOD**. He that doesn't prepare himself for eternity is a fool now forever. Is your name in the book of life?

If your name is not, just close your eyes and ask **GOD** now without hesitation. The **SPIRIT** of **GOD** will lead you.

BIBLE References:

Luk 16:19-31
Accl 12:7
Luk 16:22
Luk 15:16
Mat 17:4
Phil 4:4
Phil 3:20
Heb 12:22
Luk 15:10
1 Cor 15:44
Heb 12:24
Gen 6:10

Jam 2:26
Gen 2:7
Mat 18:2-10
2 Cor 12:2 to 4
Heb 9:27
Heb 12:22
Rev 21:27
Rev5:7 tot 14
1Thess 4:14 tot 18
Rev 24:4&5
1 Tim 2:5

Notes:

Chapter 3
Five minutes after death of a none believer

What happens to a sinner? Somebody who doesn't know the **LORD**, *minutes after his death, what does it look like on the other side? What happens there?* **JESUS** *told us in the story of the rich man and Lazarus,* **JESUS** *gave us a good indication of what happens after he died. Also with the sinner. The untruthful, the non believer, somebody who dies without salvation. We read in Luk 16:19-31 again and concentrate on the rich man. 19 "And there was" It feels real when JESUS say there was a rich man, like it really happened. "There was a certain rich man who was clothed in purple and fine linen and fared sumptuously every day. 20 But there was a certain beggar named Lazarus, full of sores, who was laid at his gate, 21 desiring to be fed with the crumbs which fell from the rich man's table. Moreover the dogs came and licked his sores. 22 So it was that the beggar died, and was carried by the angels to Abraham's bosom. The rich man also died and was buried. 23 And being in torments in Hades, he lifted up his eyes and saw Abraham afar off,*

56 | Live after Death

and Lazarus in his bosom. 24 Then he cried and said, 'Father Abraham, have mercy on me, and send Lazarus that he may dip the tip of his finger in water and cool my tongue; for I am tormented in this flame.' 25 But Abraham said, 'Son, remember that in your lifetime you received your good things, and likewise Lazarus evil things; but now he is comforted and you are tormented. 26 And besides all this, between us and you there is a great gulf fixed, so that those who want to pass from here to you cannot, nor can those from there pass to us.' 27 Then he said, 'I beg you therefore, father, that you would send him to my father's house, 28 for I have five brothers, that he may testify to them, lest they also come to this place of torment.' 29 Abraham said to him, 'They have Moses and the prophets; let them hear them.' 30 And he said, 'No, father Abraham; but if one goes to them from the dead, they will repent.'

31 ***But he said to him, 'If they do not hear Moses and the prophets, neither will they be persuaded though one rise from the dead.' "***

What happens minutes after the death of a sinner? What happens to him? **GOD'S WORD** gave us certain answers touching the end destination of humans who died and are lost. People without being saved, what happens to the sinner when he departs life?

About death, **GOD'S** clock is ticking on and the rich man had all fame, his purple and fine linen and later hangs loose off his body. And all the feasting, meals later not get touched and wasted. Then sickness comes and maybe a sick bed. After a while death knocks on your door. You see all of us have to die sooner or later, young and old, no processions or wealth stops the death. Life on earth is not eternal; the cup of joy doesn't last forever. Death has a road map which guides him to your dwelling. Death has a key to every door and fits all locks. Death doesn't show you a calendar and no excuse when he comes. For Abel death came when he was in the field, when his brother came up against him and hit him to death. For Eli as an old man sitting on a chair, for the godless Belshazzar at his own feast, with all his leaders with him. For Ananias and Safire death came in the presence of a **GOD'S** man, Peter. On the end death came to this rich man.

In Luk 16:23 *"And being in torments in Hades, he lifted up his eyes and saw Abraham afar off, and Lazarus in his bosom.* I need to remind you and maybe we have to remind ourselves regularly that death comes instantly. "The deathrate is still one per person and we all going to make it". So something unbelievable happened the man finds out minutes after death, he is not dead. Why do we always refer to five minutes after death? As mentioned in the previous chapter, most of the heart surgeons say: clinical death is when your heart stops and you are not breathing anymore, while biological death starts when all tissue died, and there are no function happening in your body.

For this reason we say death comes about 4 to 6 minutes after your heart stopped. That is what Jam 2:26 says: *"For as the body without the spirit is dead, so faith without works is dead also."*

Then we talk about the five minutes when the body and spirit separates.

This man has a shocking discovery, he is not dead, and the **BIBLE** says: *"The rich man also died and was buried. And being in torments in Hades, he lifted up his eyes"* so it means when he died he wasn't dead. The boy died and got berried, but the inner human, the spirit of the human being goes to another place. He isn't dead, and is alive but live at another place.

Minutes after his earthly death he opened his eyes, and the **BIBLE** says he was in realm of the death in verse 23 *"he lifted up his eyes"* lost people goes to realm of death, the realm of death is in the belly of the earth. In the centre of the earth, Jacob said in Gen 37:35 *"And all his sons and all his daughters arose to comfort him; but he refused to be comforted, and he said, "For I shall go down into the grave to my son in mourning." Thus his father wept for him."* And also in Num 16 we read where Moses explains what happens when people dies and goes down in the realm of death, let's read in Num 16:30 *"But if the LORD creates a new thing, and the earth opens its mouth and swallows them up with all that belongs to them, and they go down alive into the pit, then you will understand that these men have rejected the LORD." Now it came to pass, as he finished speaking all these words, that the ground split apart under them, and the earth opened its mouth and swallowed them up, with their households and all the men with Korah, with all their goods. So they and all those with them went down alive into the pit; the earth closed over them, and they perished from among the assembly."*

The new thing that **GOD** created is that these families from Korah, Dathan and Abiram that came against Moses were pushed whilst they were alive in the realm of death.

Now the rich man died first, got berried and then went to the realm of death. Then lifted his eyes and saw Lazarus against Abraham's bosom. You die before you go to the realm of death. But in this case **GOD** opened the earth and they went directly to the realm of death.

In Mat 11:23 *"And you, Capernaum, who are exalted to heaven, will be brought down to Hades; for if the mighty works which were done in you had been done in Sodom, it would have remained until this day."* With these verses in the **BIBLE** it is clear; it is down and in Mat 12:40 *"For as Jonah was three days and three nights in the belly of the great fish, so will the Son of Man"*. In Eph 4:9 the angel said: *"(Now this, "He ascended"— what it means but that He also first descended into the lower parts of the earth?"* So in this story **JESUS** gave us a clip of the happenings of the lost, the non believer. It sound so real when **JESUS** call them rich man and **HE** calls Lazarus on his name. Not in any other story **JESUS** called anybody on their name. The realm of death is in the lower parts of earth located and that is where all the souls departs to, after death.

We read in Luk 16:28 what his name is and the name have never given anywhere before this lost man in the realm of death. Read what he calls this place when he asked Abraham: 24 *"Then he cried and said, 'Father Abraham, have mercy on me, and send*

Lazarus that he may dip the tip of his finger in water and cool my tongue; for I am tormented in this flame." And then in verse 28 *"for I have five brothers, that he may testify to them, lest they also come to this place of torment."*

The realm of death is not a reality but a place: *"this place of torment."* The time of realm of death is in the heart of the earth, in depths in the under parts of earth is **GOD'S** keeping place where the lost souls, the prisoners until the last judgement of the white throne judgement. Now **JESUS** tells us what this rich man experience, the sinner, the lost man in the realm of death. In the death period many things happen.

From verse 23 the rich man got berried, like in todays live we say six foot under, and when he opened his eyes in the realm of death he was already in pain. You see after death your body goes to earth but your spirit all of a sudden is in another place, he was dead but noticed he could see, but with different eyes.

He could see how wrong he was, all his arguments, arguing cleverly whilst he was alive, and you see people who moan around you, tormented.

You also realise there is no assistance, no water and although you notice other people after death. He saw Abraham and Lazarus on the other side, so he acknowledges Abraham and knows Lazarus. The **BIBLE** is very specific: *"saw Abraham afar off and Lazarus in his bosom"* and if you have read the book "The spiritual world" it read like this "Before the crucifixion of **CHRIST** there were two large places in the realm of death. The one where the Godless people were and the other for the believers." The sinners were in the one part and **GOD'S** children in the other part. And there was a bottomless well between them and you couldn't get across this chasm. Now we know when **JESUS** died on the cross in the three days he took all the righteous souls to the paradise. But before the crucifixion you could see across to the other side, but after that it is not like that anymore. That place is empty, **JESUS** locked that place and said:"*I have the keys of Hades and of death*" after **HE** took the righteous with on his descent to heaven according to Rev 1:18. That's where the righteous is now they are in the third heaven in **GOD'S** paradise, but the sinner descents down to the realm of death.

You feel as well, see in verse 23 *"And being in torments"*. Literally the Greek "basamos" is a condition to be tormented, in other words *"tormented in flames"*. That's the man's callout in verse 24 *"Then he cried and said, 'Father Abraham, have mercy on me, and send Lazarus that he may dip the tip of his finger in water and cool my tongue; for I am tormented in this flame."* Yes it means literally to be in pain. It's not in your subconscious, it's a real feeling.

You implore for mercy and forgiveness but nobody listens; all are in the same state of torments. Then in verse 24 *"Then he cried and said, 'Father Abraham, have mercy on me,"* You are begging for water, but no one listens to you, water for your tongue. The man says in verse 24: *"and send Lazarus that he may dip the tip of his finger in water and cool my tongue;"* just a couple of minutes after death, you are in a place of torment, you long for water, and that somebody could help you and have mercy on you.

You know I just want to say this loud and clear understand this: **In the realm of death there is no mercy**, the devil is absolutely unprincipled, satan has no conscience, and he is an unprincipled liar and will do everything to pull you down into the realm of death with him.

Into pain of hell in the realm and you won't be in hell yet. Because they who are in the realm of death still have to stand in front of **GOD** according to Rev 20, that time they will be told they are sentenced to hell from the realm of death. And that is the final end judgement at the white throne of **GOD**. You can talk too, look in verse 23 *"he calls father Abraham"* all of a sudden he can speak. He calls! He pleads, now all of a sudden he wants to talk to believers, but when you were on earth you didn't want to do that, now you want to talk to **GOD**, but **GOD** does not talk to people in the realm of death. Now you want to call onto people who are **GOD'S** believers and **GOD** does not answer you.

Not only can you talk, but you can see too. And not only can you feel you can listen too. In verse 25 Abraham answers *"'Son, remember that in your lifetime you received your good things, and likewise Lazarus evil things;"* he said *"Son, remember that"* you can listen, and you can remember. What do you have to remember about this, you have to hear about all the opportunities you had, that you never took those and never got your life right with **GOD**? You also hear now it is forever too late, because Heb 9:27 *"And as it is appointed for men to die once, but after this the judgment"*.

You hear of this chasm you can't cross. You can't escape and now you were told *"remember"*, a person once said in the realm of death is the unforgettable reminder of the waisted time of life you had. So in the realm of death you have a good memory. You remember all the waisted chances you had; you remember all the calls to **GOD** and how you hardened your heart and always postponed it. You even remember your own mother's prayers for you, people who begged you to repent and change your life. You didn't listen and now it is too late, now you begin to pray and beg. Verse 27 *"I beg you therefore, father, that you would send him to my father's house"*.

In the realm of death people start to pray and beg, it could be the largest prayer service there ever will be in the realm of death, but all in vein in the realm of death, because **GOD** does not answer prayers in the realm of death. Prayer services in church people keep silent when asked to pray, people in general do not pray. Remember when you will be in the realm of death no prayer will get you out, it will be too late forever, it does not matter if you pray hourly, every minute or every second. **It will be too late.** Directly after death all call to **GOD**, without exception biggest mocker, largest antichrist or sinner. All of a sudden people become a missionary see verse 28 the rich man says: *"for I have five brothers, that he may testify to them"*.

Five minutes after death or minutes after death he begs that somebody goes out to his brothers, now he tries to make if he cares for his brothers. It is too late, you cannot try to care for people out of the realm of death, you cannot do a thing for them, and it is too late. You know after all the most frightening thing is that he was a possible Jew, an alliance child, he remembers Abraham, a Jewish form of all Christian for that time being under Abraham and called him Farther Abraham. You never thought of that even by **GOD'S** chosen Nation, nobody will be looked over, if you do not repent and follow **JESUS** and make **FATHER GOD** your **GOD** you will be casted in the realm of death for your judgement to hell.

The rich man had even a **BIBLE** and the **BIBLE** said: *"They have Moses and the prophets; let them hear them."* You can't believe they have Moses and the profits, his brothers also know the **OLD TESTAMENT**, because we know in Joh 5:45&46 "45 *Do not think that I shall accuse you to the Father; there is one who accuses you—Moses, in whom you trust. 46 For if you believed Moses, you would believe Me; for he wrote about Me. Do not think that I shall accuse you to the Father; there is one who accuses you—Moses, in whom you trust."* JESUS refers to the **BIBLE**.

Abraham's answer was in Luk 16:29 *"They have Moses and the prophets; let them hear them."* In other words they have the **BIBLE**; they have the **OLD TESTAMENT** let them read that.

They know the scriptures, they know about it and they have the preachers of **GOD'S WORD**. You can't believe if I say by means of just saying by bringing it in perspective with today's life: a church person in the realm of death? Even to own a **BIBLE** is not going to stop or save you going to the realm of death and the burning flames in hell. This man even knows of repentance, we read in verse 30 he says: *"And he said, 'No, father Abraham; but if one goes to them from the dead, they will repent".* Now he speaks out loud about repentance, and not Abraham, the rich man the sinner after his death. You know the BIBLE brought the word "repent" 240 times to us and there are still people that have never read it! This man answers: *"no Father Abraham"* and that summarises his life for me, more than everything else. He never said yes to **GOD**, his answer is "no Father Abraham" no when he was alive and no now minutes after his death in the realm of death. No when he had has good food, expensive cloths enjoying his live, then **GOD** and the **BIBLE** was not important. Unbelievable that he said no! Another thing that amazed me is this man does not have a name! This man's name was never mentioned, you know his name was not written in the book of life. Every child of **GOD'S** name says the **BIBLE** is written in the book of life. In Luk 10:20 **JESUS** said: *"but rather rejoice because your names are written in heaven."*

Phil 4:3 *"whose names are in the book of life."* And Rev 20:15 *"And whosoever was not found in the book of life was cast into the lake of fire."* Nobody will enter heaven if his name is not written in **GOD'S** book of life. You know this man had no name! Because in the realm of death you don't have a name, to be in the realm of death means you are excluded out of **GOD'S** presence, cut away from good. There will be no sympathy just burning pain, moaning and ongoing burning flames. A fire that never gets extinguished, no water, no hope of escape. There is one absolute fact in this life, your life as a believer is now the closest you will get to hell. But this: with this life it will be the closest a non believer will get to heaven. The question comes now: What about you and me? Is your name in the book of life? To go to the realm of death minutes after death without **CHRIST** will be a place of pain and suffering, and then forever in the flames of hell forever, and ever.

The words come to mind terrible, dreadful, horrible, awful, frightful, and frightening and I think fearsome describes it the best to die without **GOD** and that's the reason I just want to ask you to get things in order with the only living **GOD**. Seek **HIS** mercy and ask **HIM** to be merciful with you, and get to give **HIM** your life. Remember the script in Gen 4:10 *"And He said, "What have you done? The voice of your brother's blood cries out to Me from the ground."* And as well as the Israelites about the sins of Sodom and Gomorrah in Gen 19:12 *"like that the blood of CHRIST to GOD the judgement for all that rejected HIM"* Do you think **GOD** will forgive people rejecting **HIS SON**? Surely Heb 10:29 says: *"Of how much worse punishment, do you suppose, will he be thought worthy who has trampled the Son of God underfoot, counted the blood of the covenant by which he was sanctified a common thing, and insulted the Spirit of grace? For we know Him who said, "Vengeance is Mine, I will repay," says the Lord. And again, "The LORD will judge His people."* Do not reject the blood of **JESUS**, because that's where victory is and HIS blood gives the only forgiveness. Thank you **GOD** for forgiveness of all sins in **JESUS'S NAME**.

I beg you this minute to give yourself over to **GOD** if you are not sure if your name is written in the book of life. Even if you do it again just to make sure do it!

BIBLE References:

Luk 16:19-31
Jam 2:26
Gen 37:35
Mat 11:23
Mat 12:40
Num 16:30
Gen 37:35
Eph 4:9
2 Cor 12:23
Rev 20:23
Joh 5:46
Luk 16:29
Phil 4:3
Rev 20:15
Gen 4:10
Gen 19:12
Heb 10:29

Notes:

Chapter 4
The first resurrection

In this section we deal with the first resurrection. Read with me in the **BIBLE** and follow through as we go through this chapter. In Rev 20:5 & 6 *"But the rest of the dead did not live again until the thousand years were finished. This is the first resurrection. Blessed and holy is he who has part in the first resurrection. Over such the second death has no power, but they shall be priests of God and of Christ, and shall reign with Him a thousand years."* The second death has no power over them. There will be priests of **GOD** and **JESUS**, and will rule with **GOD** as kings a thousand years. We are looking at the first resurrection. In the previous chapter about life after death we have looked at various facts. We are at the question of what about the first resurrection? It is closely knitted with the rapture. Therefore Paul says in 1 Thess 4:16 *"And the dead in Christ will rise first"* As I understand it, those who died in **CHRIST**, the righteous on earth when **CHRIST** appears, they are the first to be resurrected. This has nothing to do with the unrighteous resurrection. When I mention the word unrighteous I want to qualify it by saying the non religious, the sinner, and we have spoken a lot about the *people that do not listen to* **GODS** *voice, they are going to hell. There is according to* **GOD'S WORD** *many good people going to hell, because the* **WORD** *says it is not by good deeds alone that gives you life in eternity with* **GOD**. *It is* **JESUS CHRIST'S** *crucifixion and death which gives you the freedom of sin and to accept* **HIM** *as your personal saviour, with you asking* **HIM** *forgiveness of your sins. That makes the difference between heaven and hell.*

When we talk about the wicket, it's not only the sinner in act, also when the godless dies without **GOD**. The first resurrection has nothing to do with the second resurrection. When we say there is a first resurrection here we see *"Blessed and holy is he who has part in the first resurrection."*

Rev 20:6 **JESUS** says that in **HIS** Word. You are blessed and holy to have part in the first resurrection.

Seeing that **HE** calls this the first resurrection it implicates that there is a second resurrection. We know the righteous will be resurrected, we know now that all will resurrect. But the unrighteous will only resurrect later, at the resurrection of judgement. The first resurrection will have judgement too. Now we read in the **BIBLE** in Rev 20 that the second resurrection will follow a thousand year later than the first resurrection. Read verse 4 *"And I saw thrones, and they sat on them, and judgment was committed to them. Then I saw the souls of those who had been beheaded for their witness to Jesus and for the word of God, who had not worshiped the beast or his image, and had not received his mark on their foreheads or* *on their hands. And they lived and reigned with Christ for a thousand years."*

WE know now the first resurrection is before the thousand years. All those resurrected need to reign with **CHRIST** a thousand years. The other death, the godless, have not resurrected before the end of the thousand years. You see the **WORD** is quite clear. The **WORD** shows us two resurrections separated with a thousand years. This places you in a privilege position to have part of the first resurrection. Remember there will be no second chance once the first resurrection takes place, either you are already dead or living when it takes place if you are not a child of **GOD**.

There are various texting in the **WORD** about the two resurrections. We read for example in 1 Cor 15:20 to 24 *"But now Christ is risen from the dead, and has become the firstfruits of those who have fallen asleep. For since by man came death, by Man also came the resurrection of the dead. For as in Adam all die, even so in Christ all shall be made alive. But each one in his own order: Christ the firstfruits, afterward those who are Christ's at His coming. Then comes the end, when He delivers the kingdom to God the Father, when He puts an end to all rule and all authority and power."* The Greek word is "Tagma" which means different divisions.

As first fruit **JESUS** and then after those belonging to **CHRIST** at **HIS** return. This is when **HE** comes to fetch **HIS** church the **WORD** said. Then the end comes.

You see there is a gap in time, because you need to consider various time restrictions. Now we read in Phil 3:8 to 12 where Paul makes this statement: *"Yet indeed I also count all things loss for the excellence of the knowledge of Christ Jesus my Lord, for whom I have suffered the loss of all things, and count them as rubbish, that I may gain Christ and be found in Him, not having my own righteousness, which is from the law, but that which is through faith in Christ, the righteousness which is from God by faith; that I may know Him and the power of His resurrection, and the fellowship of His sufferings, being conformed to His death, if, by any means, I may attain to the resurrection from the dead. Not that I have already attained, or am already perfected; but I press on, that I may lay hold of that for which Christ Jesus has also laid hold of me."* What does Paul mean by this?

It is true that all humans will resurrect. The **BIBLE** confirms that and that is according to the Christian believes a resurrection. What is the resurrection Paul strived for with strained attention to get it? It couldn't have been an ordinary resurrection, because as we said he would have been part of a resurrection in any way. There has to be this very important resurrection. So the question we are asking is why does Paul try so hard to get this specific resurrection? Well the answer is obvious. There is a resurrection that all children belong to a resurrection. See for example in Luk 20:35 & 36 **JESUS** said: *"But those who are counted worthy to attain that age, and the resurrection from the dead, neither marry nor are given* *in marriage; nor can they die anymore, for they are equal to the angels and are sons of God, being sons of the resurrection."* Because they are children of the resurrection. There is a huge difference between being a child of the judgement and to be a child of **GOD**. To be a child of the devil means you will have part of the resurrection of judgement.

To be a child of **GOD** means you will resurrect to be a child of **GOD** forever. It is quite clear that there is a framework of standards for this resurrection.

Very interesting that the children of the resurrection specifically qualified to be called children of **GOD**.

This promise is made to us in Luk 14:13 *"But when you give a feast, invite the poor, the maimed, the lame, the blind. And you will be blessed, because they cannot repay you; for you shall be repaid at the resurrection of the just."* Again the **WORD** is very specific. There is a resurrection of the children of **GOD** and that is what **GOD** says that we as believers will have part of the children of **GOD**. That's why we are children of the resurrection. The first resurrection. Now the **BIBLE** qualifies it with **JESUS** saying: *"for you shall be repaid at the resurrection of the just."* You see it is named resurrection of the righteous; it wouldn't be a general resurrection. There are defiantly two resurrections.

The different terms belongs to the first resurrection clearly showed in the **BIBLE**. Let us go through it step by step again: The first resurrection we have read about in Rev 20:6. This first resurrection will happen soon for all who die in **CHRIST**.

I just want to repeat it again: All who died in **CHRIST**, the believers who are in the Paradise in the third heaven. Following in Heb 12:23 *"to the general assembly and church of the firstborn who are registered in heaven, to God the Judge of all, to the spirits of just men made perfect,"*

Their spirit is in the presence of **GOD**. When they arrive with **CHRIST** according to 1 Thes 4 Then we who are alive and remain shall be caught up together with them in the clouds to meet the **LORD** in the sky. The body will be resurrected and join with the spirit to be a complete human again. So we who remains on earth that instant and we believe according to 1 Cor 15 that we will be part of this resurrection, will be transformed and meet up with **JESUS** in the sky. All these dead groups of people, believers have part of the first resurrection. That will happen all at ones. That's why the **BIBLE** called it the first resurrection.

This resurrection is called in Luk 20:30 the resurrection of the children of **GOD**. Against the resurrection of the godless. Against the resurrection of the other dead who did resurrect to life. Against the resurrected without **JESUS**, they who did not die in **CHRIST**. The ones who died unreligious. The ones who died unhappy. Died Godless without the **LORD** in their life.

You have the two resurrections: The resurrection of the children of **GOD** against the other resurrection. The **BIBLE** called it in Luk 20:36 the first resurrection. 1 Thes 4:16 Qualifies it a bit further that the resurrection of those died in **CHRIST**, we who is in **CHRIST** at the moment living on earth. We are already in **CHRIST** as well as those who died in **CHRIST**. In 1 Thes 4:16 and Luk 14:4 we have already seen the resurrection of the righteous. This explains it clearly that this first resurrection is defiantly for the children of **GOD**. This resurrection was described by **JESUS HIMSELF**.

The resurrection of the righteous gets described further in Heb 11:35 *"Women received their dead raised to life again. Others were tortured, not accepting deliverance, that they might obtain a better resurrection."* This resurrection is clearly just a reset to life. In other words when Elijah and other prophets of the olden days prayed that **GOD** resurrect people out of death and also through **JESUS HIMSELF**. It was just a reset to life. But we read further: The rest were filtered and didn't accept release. To receive a better resurrection, because there is a better resurrection the one of the righteous. But there is the other; the resurrection of godless. Then we read in verse 40 that **GOD** planned something better for us, where the godless will not receive the glorified body. Nobody who died before us received a glorified resurrected body, the only one who has received a glorified body is **JESUS** when **HE** resurrected out of death. Because Paul said that clearly in 1 Tim *"HE alone has immortality."* Because the first resurrection of the righteous didn't happen yet. This better resurrection didn't happen yet. Those who died already have to wait for that resurrection. The righteous are not sleeping they are in glory with **GOD**.

The first resurrection | 77

They are awaiting the resurrection, the instant unknown time of the first resurrection. Then comes their spirit with **JESUS** and will join with their body resurrecting out of the grave, and form a union again. And together lead away to meet **JESUS** in the sky. This is clearly the better resurrection.

This is defiantly the resurrection we as children are waiting for, and we know it will come soon. Rom 8:18 to 22 is also very clear in this regard.

We are all waiting for that. Paul says in verse 18 *"For I consider that the sufferings of this present time are not worthy to be compared with the glory which shall be revealed in us. For the earnest expectation of the creation eagerly waits for the revealing of the sons of God."*

"GOD'S creation was subject to futility, not willingly, but because of HIM who subjected it in hope, because the creation itself also will be delivered from the bondage of corruption into the glorious liberty of the children of God. For we know that the whole creation groans and labors with birth pangs together until now. Not only that, but we also who have the firstfruits of the Spirit, even we ourselves groan within ourselves, eagerly waiting for the adoption, the redemption of our body."

The creation is like a rolled up garment, the garment grew old, getting older every day. The earth is suffering under all things happening on the whole world, like animal types dying out, rainforests get ruined by human wrong doing. Everything else happening around the ozone layer and climate changes on earth. The creation feels deterioration and the **WORD** is describing it *"For we know that the whole creation groans and labours with birth pains together until now."***GOD** will only destroy the earth after the resurrection took place and the final judgement complete.

All happened as we read in Rev 21:23 *"But I saw no temple in it, for the Lord God Almighty and the Lamb are its temple."* Up to that moment the creations are under groans and labour every day, as we live through it.

And not only that as we read in Rom 8:23 *"Not only that, but we also who have the firstfruits of the Spirit, even we ourselves groan within ourselves, eagerly waiting for the adoption, the redemption of our body."* Our bodies will be free, how fantastic will it be, free forever. That only happens when the first resurrection took place. Or as **JESUS** described it in Joh 5:29 *"and come forth— those who have done good, to the resurrection of life, and those who have done evil, to the resurrection of condemnation."*

This resurrection which is the resurrection of the children of **GOD** alive, and the children of **GOD** who died already. The resurrection of the righteous, the better resurrection to life. This resurrection we will take part in. This first resurrection describes itself in verse Joh 5:29 *"and come forth— those who have done good, to the resurrection of life"* To accept **JESUS CHRIST** and to answer to **GOD'S** call and to live for **GOD** to satisfy **HIM**.

And then in Acts 4:2 makes the BIBLE it absolutely clear and declare as we read *"being greatly disturbed that they taught the people and preached in Jesus the resurrection from the dead."* On another place the resurrection from the dead. Exactly what Paul says when he writes about this? To preach the resurrection from the dead. The priest, the captain of the temple and the Sadducees were quite disturbed. Here we have Peter and John in the temple and preach the resurrection of JESUS CHRIST'S resurrection. Remember this follows after JESUS and it is written in that context and here they make a statement and preached the resurrection of JESUS out of the dead.

It brought a lot of trouble amongst the people, and who are they to declare the resurrection of JESUS. This is the resurrection I am talking about, and to earn this resurrection of JESUS out of the dead. Because the other death in Rev 20:5 & 6 did not come back to life. The first resurrection is out of the dead and with this the unreligious have not had a resurrection.

The resurrection of the Godless, the lost who died, those who awaits the resurrection, then the second resurrection and that will happen at the white throne resurrection. We read that in Rev 20:11 where it says: *"Then I saw a great white throne and Him who sat on it, from whose face the earth and the heaven fled away. And there was found no place for them. And I saw the dead, small and great, standing before God, and books were opened. And another book was opened, which is the Book of Life. And the dead were judged according to their works, by the things which were written in the books. The sea gave up the dead who were in it, and Death and Hades delivered up the dead who were in them. And they were judged, each one according to his works.*

Then Death and Hades were cast into the lake of fire. This is the second death." Nobody can flee away from GOD; there is no method, no manner that you can flee away from GOD. You will either be part of the first resurrection or you will be part of the second resurrection. If you are part of the first resurrection you will be safe and holy, because your name is written in the BOOK of life. You don't want to be part of the second resurrection!

BIBLE References:

Rev 20:5 en 6
1 Thess 4:16
Rev 20:6
1Cor15:20 – 24
Phil 3:8 – 12
Luk 20:35 – 36
1 Thes 4
1 Cor 15
1 Thess 4:16
Luk 14:4
Heb 11:35
1 Tim
Rom 8:18
Rev 21:23
Rom 8
Joh 5:29
Act 4:2
Rev 20:11

Notes:

Chapter 5
Glorified bodies of the righteous

Let's look at the resurrection body and what does the glorified body looks like? What we will obtain at the resurrection of the righteous. There is couple of these scripture we have to read in the BIBLE together. Open your BIBLE at Luke 24:39-43, *"39 Behold My hands"* from verse 37 this section is after JESUS'S resurrection and JESUS said to them *"39 Behold My hands and My feet, that it is I Myself. Handle Me and see, for a spirit does not have flesh and bones as you see I have. 40 " When He had said this, He showed them His hands and His feet. 41 But while they still did not believe for joy, and marveled, He said to them, "Have you any food here?* Listen to these words: *"Behold My hands and My feet, that it is I Myself."* Why does JESUS say they need to look at his hands and feet? Because the crucifixion marks is still visible, feel the wounds on my hands HE said, so you can touch a resurrected person. And HE said spirit does not have flesh and bones like you see I have. And while he said that to them he showed them his hands and feet. Whilst joyful and still didn't *believe* **HIM** *and being marvelled* **HE** *asked them do you have any food here? 42" So they gave Him a piece of a broiled fish and some honeycomb. 43 And He took it and ate in their presence."*

HE ate broiled fish with **HIS** glorified body, and some honeycomb. Now for meat lover men, **JESUS** ate fish with his glorified body and for the ladies who loves their cake, **JESUS** ate honeycomb with **HIS** glorified body. I say this with respect, but it is true; **JESUS** ate fish and honeycomb after **HIS** resurrection from death. Together with this let us read 1 Cor 15:20 *"But now Christ is risen from the dead, and has become the firstfruits of those who have fallen asleep."* **HE** was the first one who resurrected from the dead, and you may ask what about Lazarus who got up after death? And lots more in the olden days, Elijah who prayed for people and they got up out of death.

I want to state it clearly here: It was only a repair to life in the case of Lazarus, clearly not the same as **JESUS'S** glorified body's resurrection.

Christ was the first fruit who rose from the dead, and never die again, in 1 Cor 15:35 I think a general question everybody asks: How are the dead raised up? And with what body do they come? It is very informative that we will resurrect from death the same way. Rev 20:5-6 says: *"But the rest of the dead did not live again until the thousand years were finished. This is the first resurrection."* Blessed is **HE** and Holy is **HE** who has part in this first resurrection. Over such the second death has no power, but they shall be priests of **GOD** and of **CHRIST**, and shall reign with **HIM** a thousand years. I repeat blessed is he and Holy is he who has part in this first resurrection, over them the second death has no hold.

Now us who have part of the first resurrection, the second death have no power over us. You probably wonder what the second death is! In verse 14 *"Then Death and Hades were cast into the lake of fire. This is the second death."* The lake of fire the hell is the second death. Us who received the glorified body will never end up in the lake of fire, casted into hell. Thus faith in the glorified body is one of the ground rules for the Christian church, and sermons. We read in 1 Cor 15:14 *"And if Christ is not risen, then our preaching is empty and your faith is also empty."*

Our faith is not fruitless says Paul in verse 20 *"But now Christ is risen from the dead, and has become the firstfruits"* All other religions with invention religion is dead, but in the Christian religion is **Christ JESUS** alive. **CHRIST** rose out of the dead, and before I say anything about the resurrected body: We first have to mention and look at **JESUS'S** glorified body, the first; which gives us the assurance that we as children of **GOD** will also rise with a glorified body.

JESUS's glorified body: Let us look at **HIM** for a moment. We always wanted to look what a child of **GOD'S** glorified bodies would look like. The answer will definitely be, let's look at **CHRIST'S** body first. With the always question in mind: Why was **CHRIST** resurrected from death? That's the first question and for what reason? Secondly what specific meaning does **HIS** resurrection have for us?

Thirdly what does it look like and what function does **HIS** glorified body have? These are the questions I will answer first, why **JESUS** was resurrected out of death? Somebody said: It was the victory over death.

It is true that **CHRIST'S** resurrection out of death testifies beautifully of his total victory over the power of sin and death. To proof that **JESUS** had to live through a physical resurrection, and not just a spiritual resurrection, because the body is not just a temporary cover over the spirit, but belongs to the human being, because without the body Paul says humans are naked. **GOD** created the human being as a unit, soul, spirit and body and therefore saved the complete unit to be resurrected as a complete unit. In Rom 8:23 *"Not only that, but we also who have the firstfruits of the Spirit, even we ourselves groan within ourselves, eagerly waiting for the adoption, the redemption of our body."* Thus a resurrection of **JESUS'S** body wouldn't proof total victory over death and sin.

CHRIST would have had triumph over death spiritually only and not over sin, through sin separation came in death of the spirit and body, and this means without a body resurrection from death, which would affect the saved with sin remaining in **HIM**. Thus victory over death has to be set completely with the autistic reset of the unit of spirit and body. Your resurrection from the dead of the complete human being only can from a complete victory over the power of sin and death testify. That's the reason **JESUS** resurrected from death with **HIS** body. The answer on the second question why **JESUS** raised out of death is evidence that HE has total victory over sin and the power over death, but what significance has the raised out of death?

The first thing based on the most important happening is that CHRIST is the firstfruit of all passed away. CHRIST is not only resurrected out of death, to proof HIS power over death, more than that, he is the first order of resurrection the BIBLE says in 1 Cor 15:23 *"But each one in his own order: Christ the firstfruits, afterward those who are Christ's at His coming."* In other words JESUS CHRIST raised first then the large judgement will come. When Paul speaks about CHRIST as the first fruit out of death, he definitely talks about the Old Testament's reaping, that's what he had in mind.

To understand what Paul had in mind when he spoke about firstfruit, we have to go back to the Old Testament to see exactly what he spoke about, in Lev 23:10&11 *"Speak to the children of Israel, and say to them: 'When you come into the land which I give to you, and reap its harvest, then you shall bring a sheaf of the firstfruits of your harvest to the priest. He shall wave the sheaf before the LORD, to be accepted on your behalf; on the day after the Sabbath the priest shall wave it."* Now that firstfruit of the harvest the farmer had to take to the priest, he brought with faith to receive a large harvest on his land.

So the firstfruit sheaf is a guarantee that his harvest the same calibre will be, and that's why JESUS'S resurrection the guarantee and the assurance that all in CHRIST belongs or be part of the advent of CHRIST. In 1Cor 15:23 *"But each one in his own order: Christ the firstfruits, afterward those who are*

Christ's at His coming." And the BIBLE also says in Rom 8:11 *"But if the Spirit of Him who raised Jesus from the dead dwells in you, He who raised Christ from the dead will also give life to your mortal bodies through His Spirit who dwells in you."* That's the guarantee that you and I have. Then the third question, the looks of **CHRIST JESUS'S** raised body, not only why **JESUS'S** body was raised, the fact that he has total victory over the power of death and sin and what it means.

HIS resurrection out of death, in other words **HE** is the firstfruit of the harvest coming, the church, the "Iklusia", the chosen, the body of **CHRIST**, which will be raised out of death.

The harvest has to follow after the firstfruit. This is a promise that there will be a harvest, but the character of **HIS** raised body means, what **HIS** body looked like? What really helps with his sermons whilst he was on earth, there was a moment we read in Mat 17:2 in front of James, Peter and John **HE** changed appearance, and his face shined like the sun and his clothes turned as white as snow.

We can define **HIS** glorification as an external manifestation of **HIS** latent quality of **JESUS'S** resurrected body, and **HE** will keep this hidden latent quality forever exposed.

The **BIBLE** teaches us and **JESUS** said you will have the same glorified body with your resurrection as **HE** returned from the realm of death. Paul also describes it in Eph 4:9&10 *"(Now this, "He ascended"—what does it mean but that He also first descended into the lower parts of the earth? He who descended* *is also the One who ascended far above all the heavens, that He might fill all things.)"* Though JESUS'S body undergone a change with HIS reveal and maybe totally different, the inner change, whatever changes is without any doubt far above we can imagine and that the glorified body of CHRIST consisted of flesh and bones, HE declared in Luk 24:39 *"Behold My hands and My feet, that it is I Myself. Handle Me and see, for a spirit does not have flesh and bones as you see I have."*

Though JESUS'S body wasn't made of spiritual form and not bound by dust format, HE could appear as said in HIS WORD and then disappears. In Luk 24 we saw HE could go through locked doors and could appear visually next to them, and then return through the locked door as we saw in Joh 20:19 *"Then, the same day at evening, being the first day of the week, when the doors were shut where the disciples were assembled, for fear of the Jews, Jesus came and stood in the midst, and said to them, "Peace be with you."* So we can definitely see that his glorified body wasn't connected to time and bound by space, we are now ready to look what the BIBLE says what the believers glorified raised body would look like. Sure it had to be of the same quality of JESUS'S body. Let's see what Paul says what the believers glorified body will look like in 1 Cor 15:35 *"But someone will say, "How are the dead raised up? And with what body do they come?"* The resurrection out of death will be anytime through the HOLY SPIRIT. As I said above in Rom 8:23 *"But if the Spirit of Him who raised Jesus from the dead dwells in you,"* Then will HE that raised JESUS out of death also bring our mortal bodies alive? In any way the quality of the body which will be the same as **JESUS'S** glorified body. Paul proves that when he wrote to the Philippians and the Romance.

In Phil 3:20&21 *"For our citizenship is in heaven, from which we also eagerly wait for the Savior, the Lord Jesus Christ, who will transform our lowly body that it may be conformed to His glorious body, according to the working by which He is able even to subdue all things to Himself."* We expect the **LORD JESUS CHRIST** who will change our humiliating body, earthly body and to be the same as **HIS** glorified body as in Rom 8:29 and this he previously order to be equal to **GOD'S SON**. So we have these two cases.

Our humiliated body will be transformed by **JESUS** to be equal to **HIS** glorified body. We will receive the same glorified body as **JESUS CHRIST** at our resurrection. It was always **GOD'S** plan for us forever. Paul says in Rom 8:29 that **GOD** organised us to have the same glorified body equal to **HIS SON**. Not as **JESUS**, because we can't be all **JESUS**, there is only one **JESUS**. But there will be many with the same glorified body. I mean like John confirm it when he writes in 1 Joh 3:2 *"Beloved, now we are children of God; and it has not yet been revealed what we shall be, but we know that when He is revealed, we shall be like Him, for we shall see Him as He is."* We shall see **JESUS** as **SON** of **GOD** one day when we see **HIS** glorified body. The **BIBLE** say:

We know when **HE** reveals **HIMSELF** the day **HE** comes back to earth, every eye will see **HIM**, and we will be changed and have a glorified body equal to **HIS**. The same conformity.

The same glorified body, because we will see **HIM** as **HE** is. What a **GODLY** wonderful promised for people always sick in their bodies, people with lost limbs, people with struggle, and some people who's lost a limb in an accident. Just think of that: There will be a perfect glorified body that **GOD** prepared for you forever. This reborn body is the part equal to **JESUS CHRIST'S** glorified body. Though he held his identity the body and bones changed and will be different to what we know now in today's life. Now 1 Cor 15 the only chapter in the **BIBLE** which clarifies the risen and glorified body. Paul gives us four characteristics of the glorified body. Firstly: Take note it will be incorrupt, in verse 42 Paul declare *"So also is the resurrection of the dead. The body is sown in corruption, it is raised in incorruption."* Sown in dishonor and raised in glory. This body will not determinate or weaken, because it is exalted above death like in Rom 6:5 *"For if we have been united together in the likeness of His death, certainly we also shall be in the likeness of His resurrection,"* Praise the **LORD**. When I die with **JESUS** in my life, I will be equal to **HIS** resurrection and will have the same resurrected body. So it will be imperishable, what is that: an always reminder of a mark of the resurrected body.

Secondly: 1 Cor 15:43 *"It is sown in dishonor, it is raised in glory. It is sown in weakness, it is raised in power."* Paul says it is raised in glory. So when he says it is sown in dishonor, weakness he maybe means miss form, paraplegic, but the resurrected body will be raised in power and glory. Many people doesn't know what the word glory means, it is the Greek word "doska" and means literally the visual manifestation of hidden quality of the secrecy of the body. We can illustrate it with a white light. What is the magnificence and hidden quality of a white light?

If we break it up through a prism the hidden colours of the rainbow shows. The real colours shows. Now our glorified body will reflect the same colours. This resurrected body will show its powerful glare of light and be manifested that specific day and will be the same as JESUS'S body when HE comes. Let us read what Daniel wrote about that in Dan 12:3 *"Those who are wise shall shine Like the brightness of the firmament, And those who turn many to righteousness Like the stars forever and ever."*

The third characteristic is the resurrected body is a powerful body, it said in

1 Cor 15:43 *"It is sown in weakness, it is raised in power."* The body won't be bound by the earthly. There will be no more fatigue, where no exhaustion be noticed. Your renewed glorified body will have no deteriation in strength forever. And then finally Paul explains in 1 Cor 15:44 that your body will be a spiritual body too *"It is sown a natural body, it is raised a spiritual body. There is a natural body, and there is a spiritual body."* What does the BIBLE mean with a natural body?

It doesn't mean the same than the glorified body, made of spirit, that it won't have any substance; it will have all in one but not like the earthly body now.

We know it is a body with flesh and bone as JESUS declared in Luk 24:39 and it is visible and tangible. Also that the glorified body and spiritual body is all in one and under the control of the **HOLY SPIRIT** such a spirit filled life will be free of the restrictions we have in our bodies now. Every now and then the question arises; with what body will none believers be resurrected? Who never accepted JESUS as their saviour, the unrighteous will have a body that dies again. The other dead Rev 20:5 did not rise until the 1000 years come too passed, and will stay forever in the pernicious. We read in Isai 66:23 & 24 that their resurrected bodies will be thrown in the fire, because that body can die again. The none believer does not have the triumph as the believer, and every month on the new moon as said in Isai 66:23&24

"And it shall come to pass that from one New Moon to another, and from one Sabbath to another, all flesh shall come to worship before Me," says the LORD. "And they shall go forth and look upon the corpses of the men who have transgressed against Me. For their worm does not die, and their fire is not quenched. They shall be abhorrence to all flesh."

It could be that this place mentioned be the pool of fire visible to all people on earth as a monument of **GOD'S** justice forever. The **GODLY'S** body will be forever immortal and the non believer forever horrible as Daniel said in Dan 12:2 *"some to shame and everlasting contempt."* JESUS declares in Mat 25:46 "and these" this is the godless" will go away into everlasting punishment, but the righteous into eternal life." The righteous will have a wonderful inherited life in a glorified body with the **LORD JESUS** in heaven forever. The non righteous will be without **GOD** with a body that dies, but still have mortal bodies which will burn in the fire of hell. Again **JESUS** verifies that the non righteous will be casted in hell. He said in Mat 5:30 *"And if your right hand causes you to sin, cut it off and cast it from you; for it is more profitable for you that one of your members perish, than for your whole body to be cast into hell."*

Thereon I plead with you now, make sure that you have accepted the **LORD JESUS** as you personal saviour, then you will for sure be given a glorified body. Free of death, free of the power of sin and with total victory.

BIBLE References:

Lukas 24:39-43
Rev 20: 5-6
Rom 8:23
Lev 3:10+11
Mat 17:2
Joh 20:19
Rom 8:29
Rom 6:5
1 Cor 15:43
Dan 12:3
Asa 66:23, 24
Dan 12:2
Mat 25:46
Mat 5:30

1 Cor 15:20
1 Cor 15:14
1 Cor15:23
Rom 8:11
Eph 4: 9+10
1 Cor 15:35
1 Joh 3:2

Notes:

Chapter 6
Problems with death texting

The theme we talk about now is: Where is the death? Problematic texting we know about what happens after death. There are a couple sections we will discuss. Problematic texting in the **BIBLE** about life after death. All attention on the following: Eph 4:8-10 *"Therefore He says: When He ascended on high, He led captivity captive, and gave gifts to men." (Now this, "He ascended"—what does it mean but that He also first descended into the lower parts of the earth? He who descended is also the One who ascended far above all the heavens, that He might fill all things.)"*

The discussion hereof is what happened when **JESUS** died on the cross? And the three days after **HIS** death on the cross, before **HE** rose from the death with **HIS** glorified body and appeared to **HIS** disciples that night. The resurrection night, and we know it was on a Sunday night according to the **BIBLE**. In Joh 20:19 *"The first day of the week."* So **JESUS** rose on the

Sunday, and the main reason we are gathering for church services on a Sunday as the first day of the week. Now the first question asked? When he rose to the heavens capture the captive and took them with him. Who are these captives? Then this proposition in Eph 4:9 *"HE decented to heavens - What else does it mean that HE first ascended to the lower parts of the earth. HE who descended is also the ONE who ascended far above all the heavens,"* HE took a group of people with HIM before HE descended to heavens. The realm of death undergone a huge change after his death and ascend.

In the previous chapter we already spoke about the spiritual world, about the realm of death and life after death, we have referred to this in that respect. But there are certain things we haven't touched.

We are going through that now. Remember when **CHRIST** raised after three days being in the realm of death, HE didn't rose alone.

We read in Eph 4:8 *"When HE ascended on high, HE led captivity captive, and gave gifts to men."* But HE first ascended before HE descended.

The question is what is the **BIBLE** telling us here? Isn't it that the paradise section was emptied? And that all the righteous from Adam to **JESUS'S** resurrection were moved to the paradise in heavens with **HIM**. Paul confirmed that when he had the experience close to death when he was stoned by the Jews and dragged outside the city to die. However when the disciples gathered around him he rose up and went into the city. Now in 2 Cor 12:2 to 4 Paul explained word for word what happened then. *"I know a man in Christ who fourteen years ago—whether in the body I do not know, or whether out of the body I do not know, God knows—such a one was caught up to the third heaven. And I know such a man—whether in the body or out of the body I do not know, God knows— how he was caught up into Paradise and heard inexpressible words, which it is not lawful for a man to utter."* Paul says the paradise is in the third heaven now. All righteous, from the **OLD TESTAMENT** times up to **JESUS's** crucifixion. All the believers who were in the heart of the earth, now with the resurrection of **JESUS** transferred to the third heaven and it is interesting that **JESUS** depopulated the paradise side of the realm of death in the heart of the earth. Taken that part to the third heaven and locked the other part.

We read in Rev 1:18 *"I am He who lives, and was dead, and behold, I am alive forevermore. Amen. And I have the keys of Hades and of Death."* **Jesus** has the power and the authority over death, and has the keys of hades. The **BIBLE** also declares in 1 Sam 2:6 *"The LORD kills and makes alive; He brings down to the grave and brings up."* What a testimony that the **LORD** decides who dies and is casted to the hades or to the third heaven.

We also know the parable between the rich man and Lazarus, with Abraham in the life after death. Before the crucifixion Luke 16 reads "26 *And besides all this, between us and you there is a great gulf fixed, so that those who want to pass from here to you cannot, nor can those from there pass to us."*

It means one group on the one side and the second group on the otherwise of the hades. When **JESUS** died on the cross and ascent to the side where Lazarus was, where all **GOD'S** believers was. Then the paradise side were taken up to heaven. Where most of our love ones are and all the believers. If ever the question arises: Where is my loved ones? I know now they are localised in paradise in the highest heaven. Also means they are with **LOVELY JESUS CHRIST** and our **HEAVENLY FATHER**.

We hear often that the spirits of the deceased people are called up by mediums. We looked at television programs "On the other side of death" or "Crossing over" that so many people boast that they can communicate with love ones and could pass messages over to them. With this I want to make it very clear to you that the spirits of the deceased people cannot be called up by mediums. We as Christians believe in **GOD**, the **BIBLE**. The ones that died in **JESUS** are in heaven. We can't call them from heaven, out of paradise and to communicate with them and to ask them how they are, and if they are safe and in a place of rest is. Never the less can we speak to the ones who died outside of **CHRIST**. They who died as sinners, died as the lost. We cannot communicate with them, the **BIBLE** say: **AVOID WICKED CUSTOMS**. Lets read and hear what the **LORD** said about that in Deut 18:9 to 14 *"When you come into the land which the LORD your God is giving you, you shall not learn to follow the abominations of those nations. There shall not* *be found among you anyone who makes his son or his daughter pass through the fire, or one who practices witchcraft, or a soothsayer, or one who interprets omens, or a sorcerer, or one who conjures spells, or a medium, or a spiritist, or one who calls up the dead.*

For all who do these things are an abomination to the LORD, and because of these abominations the LORD your God drives them out from before you. You shall be blameless before the LORD your God. For these nations which you will dispossess listened to soothsayers and diviners; but as for you, the LORD your God has not appointed such for you."

You see we cannot consult with the dead! It is forbidden by **GOD the CREATOR, because who do these things is an abomination to the LORD.** People who communicates through mediums, on behalf of you, try to communicate with the dead communicate with daemons and evil non **GODLY** spirits. They do have information of our loved ones, like for example most of them knew what happened to our family members when alive on earth. Though every time they consult through a medium, they will say: your father is dead, and died in a motor accident, remembers your sister or brother this and that and had this imaginary complaint. And at his stage he lost his finger and this one was there by the birth of that one, and or this is what happened in the past. Then at that stage as you can hear by trickery people will believe the mediums.

Because he mentioned something correctly, when they make these propositions. Because people accept things, because the medium has some things correct, they accept all the rest of rubbish they are told and believe it is correct. The mediums only know of true happenings. It is only evil spirits transferring to the mediums. We know now **GOD** does not let us do that. You cannot communicate with the dead. People can communicate with evil spirits and deamons; it is possible because the devil would like you to do just that, to break your link with the **HOLY SPIRIT**. We call that Satanism, channeling or whatever new age terms people are using today. **GOD** forbids his children to do that. We are not permitted to have your hand palms read, or calling the dead for guidance, specifically for things in the future, or viewing of leaves in a tea cup to predict the future.

And the evil crystal ball and pendulum and all the man made board games to make contact with the underworld. We are forbidden and can only make contact though JESUS with the only true SPIRIT, the **HOLY SPIRIT** of **GOD**, to have such a relationship with **GOD** through **HIS SPIRIT**. The compartment where all the non religious spirits are kept up to the judgment day is still in the underworld. It means in life after death, people who died, is dead but their spirits is at a different place. The spirit lives and remains in the realm of death where the unrighteous and those lost souls who died.

Without **GOD**. With death of the Godless his spirit still goes to the hates localised in the underworld. After the 1000 years of freedom according to Rev 20 these dead will be called up to **GOD'S** judgment. John writes in Rev 20:13 & 14 *"The sea gave up the dead who were in it, and Death and Hades delivered up* *the dead who were in them. And they were judged, each one according to his works. Then Death and Hades were cast into the lake of fire. This is the second death."* It is very clear that the dead outside **CHRIST** in the hades goes to the judgment in front of **GOD**. Verse 11 says: *"Then I saw a great white throne"* as the heading says above verse 11 **THE GREAT WHITE THRONE JUDGEMENT**. Those people have to stand before **GOD** and be judged according to their works.

Now another problematical text occurring every time you read it, and many students argue about, is the life after death in Mat 27: 52-53 *"and the graves were opened; and many bodies of the saints who had fallen asleep were raised; and coming out of the graves after His resurrection, they went into the holy city and appeared to many."* Now the question comes: Who were those people? Verse 50 said: *"And Jesus cried out again with a loud voice, and yielded up His spirit. Then, behold, the veil of the temple was torn in two from top to bottom; and the earth quaked, and the rocks were split,"* This is naturally a huge force.

Because that veil of the temple was about 100mm thick and will take a large group of ox to tear the veil when pulled in both directions. The **BIBLE** said when **JESUS** died the veil torn in half in the **HOLY** and **ALL HOLY** sections, torn from the top to bottom. It was a **GODLY** miracle that took place in the temple. **GOD** tears the veil in **HIS** temple which leads to **HIS HOLYNESS** when **JESUS'S** body torn on the cross and yielded up **HIS** spirit. The veil torn, in verse 52*"and the graves were opened; and many bodies of the saints who had fallen asleep* *were raised; Then, behold, the veil of the temple was torn in two from top to bottom; and the earth quaked, and the rocks were split, and coming out of the graves after His resurrection, they went into the holy city and appeared to many."*

The question is: Who are they? Many of them revealed fiscically in Jerusalem to many people. Again the question who were they? These people must have died recently just after the three day period, just before **JESUS** was resurrected, like Lazarus in Joh 11:43-44 we read how Lazarus died and after four days **JESUS** stood at the outside of his grave and called " *Lazarus come out!*" After Lazarus was in the grave already four days and started to smell the **BIBLE** said, he was resurrected out of death. He was healed and *"Now when He had said these things, He cried with a loud voice, "Lazarus, come forth!" And he who had died came out bound hand and foot with grave clothes, and his face was wrapped with a cloth. Jesus said to them, "Loose him, and let him go."* This was just a revival similar like the prayer the profit brought the child to life in 1 Kings 17and just like **JESUS** brought people in Luk 8 to life. It was definitely just a bringing back to life. Those people were definitely known by their people in Jerusalem. It couldn't have been people who died ages ago; it doesn't make sense to reveal them in public. Nobody would have recognised them living before their generation. The bothering question is still: Are they resurrected like **JESUS** out of the death with a glorified body and are they together with **JESUS** the firstborn, the first fruit out of death? That would have been an important question to ask.

Problems with death texting | 105

These people we read of in Mat 27:52(Mark 15:21-41, Luk 23:26-49, Joh 19:17-37) *"and coming out of the graves after His resurrection, they went into the holy city and appeared too many. And the graves were opened; and many bodies of the saints who had fallen asleep were raised;"* the day JESUS died on the cross, three days after that they appeared in the streets and went into the city Jerusalem and to many people. It must have been a rare event in history of the earth. Not only JESUS appeared, but many other people and appeared to their loved ones in the city. The question remains: Did they resurrect with glorified bodies like JESUS? Or were their appearance just a revival? We are making an assumption it was just a revival before they departed with JESUS to heaven.

The BIBLE gives specific announcement about this when Paul wrote to Timothy in 1Tim 6: 14&15

"that you keep this commandment without spot, blameless until our Lord Jesus Christ's appearing, which He will manifest in His own time, He who is the blessed and only Potentate, the King of kings and Lord of lords, "who alone has immortality, dwelling in unapproachable light, whom no man has seen or can see, to whom be honor and everlasting power. Amen." It is quite clear that JESUS CHRIST is the only one here with immortality. The only thing we can say about this is that these people didn't have glorified bodies like JESUS, but revived to life like Lazarus and the other we read off in the BIBLE. They relive and couldn't be the firstfruit sheaf like JESUS CHRIST out of death. JESUS alone is the firstfruit from death. Our

guarantee is that one day we will rise the day JESUS come again and will then be resurrected with a glorified body just like his. The complexity of this text is not that difficult if we read it in conjunction with the whole BIBLE. These people appeared to others in the city. It wouldn't have meant anything if they were unknown to the people in the city. It is obvious that they recently died before JESUS'S crucifixion. It must have been close to JESUS'S death.

We just need to look ahead a bit, the paradise were in the third heaven and that the Old Testament's paradise was in the realm of death before and after JESUS'S resurrection now transferred to heaven.

It is clear and prominent that we are not reading in the BIBLE anything of the righteous after death going down to the hates. You have to come to grips what the BIBLE says that no child of GOD will go down but, rise into heaven. You can't go down; you can only decent to heaven after death. Paul writes to the Corinthians in 2 Cor 5:8 *"We are confident, yes, well pleased rather to be absent from the body and to be present with the Lord."* They do not live in the realm of death, the live in heaven. In Phil 1:23 *"For I am hard-pressed between the two, having a desire to depart and be with Christ, which is far better."* Now where is CHRIST?

When Stephan was stoned as written in Act 7:55 we read he looked up towards heaven and said I have looked in heaven and seen CHRIST sitting on the right of GOD the FATHER.

You can't unconsciously be with **JESUS** in the paradise, got to be the most precious experience and feeling ever felt. So the **BIBLE** teaches us we will depart to the **GLORY** of **GOD** when we die. Paul said in Phil 1:23 *"For I am hard-pressed between the two, having a desire to depart and be with Christ, which is far better."* So it will be the best by far. We know now that we will be in the paradise after death and all our loved ones will be there. In 1 Thes 4:13 to 18 *"But I do not want you to be ignorant, brethren, concerning those who have fallen asleep, lest you sorrow as others who have no hope. For if we believe that Jesus died and rose again, even so God will bring with Him those who sleep in Jesus. For this we say to you by the word of the Lord, that we who are alive and remain until the coming of the Lord will by no means precede those who are asleep. For the Lord Himself will descend from heaven with a shout, with the voice of an archangel, and with the trumpet of God. And the dead in Christ will rise first.*

Then we who are alive and remain shall be caught up together with them in the clouds to meet the Lord in the air. And thus we shall always be with the Lord. Therefore comfort one another with these words."

We remaining on earth will change in an instant according to 1 Cor 15:51 to 53 *"Behold, I tell you a mystery: We shall not all sleep, but we shall all be changed— in a moment, in the twinkling of an eye, at the last trumpet. For the trumpet will sound, and the dead will be raised incorruptible, and we shall be changed. For this corruptible must put on incorruption, and this mortal must put on immortality. So when this corruptible has put on incorruption, and this mortal has put on immortality, then shall be brought to pass the saying that is written: "Death is swallowed up in victory."*

In 1 Thes 4:3 *"But I do not want you to be ignorant, brethren, concerning those who have fallen asleep, lest you sorrow as others who have no hope."* We will descent with **JESUS** in the sky. Firstly the believers will be prepared to be ready to go anywhere in heaven. Somebody said once: "Heaven is a prepared place for prepared people".

JESUS said I am going to prepare a place for you and when **I** am finish I will come and take you there to be with **ME** because I am in heaven. Then we will go into our heritage immortal, pure and not faded. Like Peter wrote in 1 Pet 1:4 *"to an inheritance incorruptible and undefiled and that does not fade away, reserved in heaven for you,"* what a wonderful thought of our awaiting new home. Paul said what the eye not seen, what the ear not heard and never came up in the heart of men, what **GOD** prepared for him who loves **HIM**. We a wonderful life awaits us as children of the only living **GOD**.

BIBLE References:

Eph 4:8-10
Act 14:19 to 20
2 Cor 12:2-4
Rev 1:18
1 Sam 2:6
Deut 18:9
Rev 20:13&14
Mat 27: 52-53   Mar 15:21-41   Luk 23:26-49   Joh 19:17-37
Joh 11:43-44
1 King 17
Luk 8
1 Tim 6: 14&15
2 Cor 5:8
Phi 1:23
1 Thes 4:13-18
1 Cor 15:51-53
1 Pet 1:4

Notes:

Chapter 7
The judgement-seat of JESUS

We are now going to look at you, child of **GOD** appearing before the judgement chair of **JESUS CHRIST**. *This takes place in life after death.* The **BIBLE** is very clear on this and explains it in many words in 2 Cor 5:10 *"For we must all appear"* and I need to qualify that Apostle Paul is talking about the religious, not about the sinners. *The sinners will appear another time before another judgement whereof I will tell you about in the next chapter.* *"For we must all appear"* as believers *"before the judgement seat of CHRIST, that each one may receive the things done in the body, according to what he has done, whether good or bad."* It means every child of **GOD** have to stand before the judgement chair of **CHRIST**, not before **GOD** or the **HOLY SPIRIT** but appear before the judgement chair of **CHRIST**. *Paul repeats himself when he wrote to the Romans, and surely it was for them too, he says in Rom 14:8 to 10 "**But why do you judge your brother?**" You see he is talking to the religious and not the sinners.*

But for the children of the LORD he says: *"But why do you judge your brother? Or why do you show contempt for your brother? For we shall all stand before the judgment seat of Christ. For it is written: As I live, says the LORD, every knee shall bow to Me, and every tongue shall confess to God."* You see then each of us shall give account of himself to **GOD**. So we have to give account before the judgement seat of **JESUS**. He says in many words in verse 10 *"For we shall all stand before the judgement seat of CHRIST."* Take note, this is important everybody have to prepare himself that will be a time that you will appear before the judgement seat as child of **GOD**. The person who misses the judgement seat of **JESUS**, in other words all die without **CHRIST**, the sinner who is lost, everybody in the realm of death, under in the body of earth.

Those people who died without being saved will appear before the "**WHITE THRONE**" Rev 20:11 says very specifically

"Then I saw a great white throne and Him who sat on it, from whose face the earth and the heaven fled away. And there was found no place for them." But surely we as Christians know we are not fleeing away from **GOD** we are fleeing to **HIM**.

But those who died without the **LORD** have to appear before the white throne. This is it, we cannot change **GOD'S WORD**, neither the future nor no prophetical **WORD** or prophesy against, and we cannot ignore **GOD'S WORD**. These words are there "every living creature will appear before **GOD** on the day **HE** determined it." That day is two days apart from the first judgement. That day the created will face his **CREATOR** and look

HIM in the eyes. That day every human being will see **GOD**. That will be a day of all days ever existed. If we think of what Daniel 12:1 said about that day, *"some to everlasting life, some to shame and everlasting contempt."* He sees it as two different happenings. The one: where some will enter everlasting life and second: shame and everlasting contempt.

For the purpose of this discussion I just want to pull your attention on the "Bhma" in a Greek term which means the judgement seat of **JESUS**. I just want to explain to you how a religious here on earth looks like in this regard. We read it in the **BIBLE** and I just want to explain what it means to stand at the judgement seat of **CHRIST**.

We read in 1 Cor 3:10 *"According to the grace of God which was given to me, as a wise master builder I have laid the foundation, and another builds on it. But let each one take heed how he builds on it. For no other foundation can anyone lay than that which is laid, which is Jesus Christ. Now if anyone builds on this foundation with gold, silver, precious stones, wood, hay, straw, each one's work will become clear; for the Day will declare it, because it will be revealed by fire; and the fire will test each one's work, of what sort it is."*

Good let's talk about the appearance before the judgement seat. We must never forget we are not only on our way to glory, but will also face judgement. You and I know that now.

Just think about this life is a huge challenge, because this one life we have determines our life after death forever, if I receive a crown from **CHRIST** or will I lose the crown supposedly meant for us by **GOD**. Now the judgement seat: the child of **GOD** does not go to the white throne. We are going to the judgement seat of **CHRIST**. Remember the religious goes to the judgement seat. The core thought of the judgement seat in **GOD'S WORD** was always a place of reward. When we look at 2 Cor 5:10 and Rom 14:8 to 10 and 1 Cor 3:10 it is the judgement of reward, but Revelations has to do with the white throne judgement with no reward only sentence to hell. If we can divide the two things for a moment, the first reward, and the second punishment.

Let's look at the child of GOD judgement, then the white throne where we look at the judgement which is the end result of hell. The judgement seat is the test against your works, if it is spiritual or fleshly, if there is reward or rejection. The **BIBLE** is clear about that. If some bodies work sustain against the fire he will get a reward, and if their works burnt out like hay they will suffer loss. It means and I have to remind myself: I can compare it with two things in my life; I can firstly build my life with things of value lasting forever or something not valuable that will burn out in the test of fire. Things of value for **GOD** and not necessary of human's importance. The reward will be a crown something of endless value. Remember you will rule with your crown.

The **BIBLE** explains clearly what you should use to build. Gold, silver, precious stones, wood, hay and straw. Now in 1 Cor 3:12 *"Gold, silver and precious stones"* represents what **GOD** had in mind as valuables for your life. When gold, silver and precious stones get melted through fire you will have a billet of gold. By mining and braking up the rocks into smaller segments the precious metals gets extracted and then smelted under high temperatures, then getting poured as a liquid into a mould.

With this heat and additives all the scale floats on top and only the pure gold remains in this beautiful gold bar. This block of gold has a high value as we know, and by human nature we overspend money buying gold articles. What's going to happen: When we are at the judgement chair the gold, silver and the precious stones, these which are valuable before **GOD**, the **BIBLE** calls that good works of the religious.

JESUS CHRIST HIMSELF will evaluate each child of **GOD'S** contribution for **HIS** kingdom. **HE** is going to evaluate the works by putting it through the test of fire, it says in the **WORD** everyone's work will come to light. That day will show and revealed by fire. The fire will proof everybody's works.

No matter how small it is as said in verse 13 *"each one's work will become clear; for the Day will declare it, because it will be revealed by fire; and the fire will test each one's work, of what sort it is. If anyone's work which he has built on it endures, he will receive a reward."* The judgement seat judgement will reveal the true motives of each child of GOD. Hence the reason Paul said in 1 Cor 4:5

"Therefore judge nothing before the time, until the Lord comes, who both will bring to light the hidden things of darkness and reveal the counsels of the hearts. Then each one's praise will

come from God." That was what he said about the test of fire. No gain in blindly judging people left and right, about what they are doing for **GOD** and the values of it.

You don't know the people totally like our **CREATOR**, to judge and say their life means nothing for **GOD**. What do I know what's in the heart of people and what they do in **GOD'S** eyes? There are people who do tremendous valuable things for **GOD'S** work. Many people tries to show off to all about their deeds and to be on all peoples lips about their things they do for their church, but that is not what **GOD** want and means nothing to **GOD**. That day when all motives will be revealed and come before the test of fire, the truth will be revealed.

The word "good works" means lack of time, means damage forever. So everybody's works will endeavour the fire of **CHRIST** how small it is. When your works stood up you will receive an award, and if your works burns out you will loose out. There is a forever lost for the child of **GOD** whose works can't stand in the fire test.

The **BIBLE** also tells us in 1 Cor 3:12 about the term of the loosing works and calls it "wood, hay and straw".

In the one hand gold, silver and precious stones and in the other hand wood, hay and straw. You know when you throw wood, hay or straw in a fire it gets consumed immediately and burn to ash instantly. I just want to emphasize what the **BIBLE** says about your loss building your foundation on consumables.

In verse 10 it says: *"Let each one take heed now how he builds on it."* And in verse 11 it says: *"For no other foundation can anyone lay than that which is laid, which is JESUS CHRIST."* Everything you have built without **JESUS** has no value. All your work for **HIS** kingdom, what you have done for his eklusia "the body of **CHRIST**" and individuals in **CHRIST** that is what counts. Not peoples valuations through their mouth, but by **GOD**. Where **GOD** was praised and honoured, glorified before **HIM** alone. That is what I am talking about, not your glory and your praises, but only by **GOD**. That is the gold, silver and precious stone what **GOD** talks about.

The other is the wood, hay and straw will bring only loss and no gain. All your works you thought were so wonderful, which I thought was so important to me, means nothing. Then we are untruthful builders. In other words we are sitting in a position with no choice but doing what **GOD** said we should do for **HIM**. If I do what I think I should do it will all go up in flames. You have to look at your life again and reconsider what we are doing for **CHRIST**. Let's go to Mat 16:27 *"For the Son of Man will come in the glory of His Father with His angels, and then He will reward each according to his works."* You got to hear this clearly! Your works! Even in the last **BOOK** of the **BIBLE GOD** warned us with **HIS** last words.

You as child of **GOD** he warns you in Rev 22:12 *"And behold, I am coming quickly, and My reward is with Me, to give to every one according to his work."* How do you build and with what are you building? We are privileged to work for **GOD** to have the opportunity to stand before the judgement seat to get judged by our good works and know with what we have to build and know to build on **JESUS** the cornerstone of our faith.

Everyone have a part and occupation in **GOD'S** works for **HIS** kingdom and if we are faithful to this works **HE** has put us in, which will follow with:

The rapture will happen in the beginning of the seven year period of oppression, when **JESUS** will meet us in the sky and take us with to the judgement seat for **HIS** judgement test, where our works will be tested by fire.

When the seven years takes place on earth you will be called in front of the judgement seat. The **BIBLE** talks about the large oppression that will take place on earth in Mat 24 and Rev 7.

The point I want to make is the following: In that seven years the judgement seat will take place in heaven. The judge is **JESUS CHRIST**, and the people the believers, the time are after the rapture in the seven years of oppression. The place is in heaven at the judgement seat of **JESUS** and by the basis of his works and **JESUS** will sit on the throne on the judgement seat and the result will be the following: **HE** will hand out rewards. Honest and fair to whom **HE** considers and there will be millions getting a reward or crown the **BIBLE** says, to all **HIS** children. It is qualified in 1 Cor 3 to whose works not standing in the test will lose reward. You are saved because you are standing in heaven in front of **JESUS**, you are not lost. I just want to say this to you clearly **GOD'S WORD** says even all your works doesn't give you reward that instant you are still safe in heaven and has nothing to do with your salvation.

You are **HIS** child, you are there, and cannot lose your salvation in the process. But remember this is the test of your life and you are now busy to prepare yourself for your reward.

Your character now, how you serve **GOD** now with your Christian work and your Christian labour in **GOD'S** work now, because we know it is not the end. But we know you still need to be tested and the quality to be determined by **JESUS** our **GOD**. At the moment there is a vale over our Christian works on earth until that day in 1 Cor 3:13 the "Bhma" The judgement seat of **JESUS** take place.

That day when **JESUS** removes the vale of HIS bride your works and then reveals it like only **GOD** our **CREATOR HIMSELF** can show in truth. That will be our final test for eternity.

How **JESUS** will do that, it will be done by fire the **WORD** said. The fire won't attempt the people, you won't go through fire, it will be your works. Thank **GOD** the fire is not meant for you. The fire of hell is for the white throne judgment, and they stay at the white throne judgment, all whose name is not written in the Book of Life. Rev 20:14 "*Then death and hades were cast into the lake of fire.*" But for the religious his works will be tested with fire, you see the difference between the two clearly.

When you gave your heart for **GOD**, the fire will consume many of your works, yes it is true, but the hard worker will be saved.

The test will be a thorough test and everything will be investigated. The **CHRIST** test will be perfect and nothing will be hidden from **HIM** and stand before **HIM**, **HIS** eyes the **BIBLE** said **HIS** eyes are like a consuming fire and **HE** will sit on **HIS** throne and judge. **HE** will test the fire **HIMSELF**. **HE** loves the truth and hate lies. That day will bring to light what the truth of your works is, of your complete life. Yes we can test ourself, it isn't that difficult to run a self test. You can ask yourself what this test will consist off. Somebody had a dream about the **CHRIST** test and wrote it down as follows:

GOD doesn't say it in so many words. "The man said he had a dream and stood before the judgment seat of **CHRIST** and what he learnt from this test. About how he knew the **WORD** and how he explained the scriptures.

And when he understood it, the effort he has done and discovered it with all falseness and all the things he participate in, and when the judgment come he only received 5 persent. His jealousy 9 percent and lawfulness and criticizing were 7 percent.

You see all these things were wood, hay and straw, all these things added up; his hypocrisy, his discord he created, his personal ambition, his personal flesh 10 percent each.

His commitment to his church, and attitude my church is correct and all other churches are wrong. There was 8 percent for his own talents, and did these things and those things and only gave him 11 percent. Liked to control other people and when he saw all added up he received 91 percent wasted with his life; burnt as wood, hay and straw.

But his love for **GOD** was only 4 percent and his love for his neighbours was only 3 percent. His commitment to do **GOD'S** works only 2 percent and realised he only had 9 percent, only 9 percent of his whole life gave him his reward. This means 91 percent was destroyed." Now you and I know this was just a dream this person had, but the reality is there, we as humans can add our life up and soon you will make a discovery that we only have 9 percent left over for a reward. Children of **GOD** who proposed themselves as children of **GOD**, but is so far away from **GOD**. Weigh your life and works up today child of **GOD** and start today in all seriousness and honesty to ask the **HOLY SPIRIT** to show you how to improve your works of **GOD**, when you stand in front of this living **GOD** that your works will give you a higher reward. Nobody will flee away with this judgement of **JESUS** but your works will give you the ultimate reward. We need to live our life that your life will bring a huge profit for **GOD'S KINGDOM**. You will only smile when you hear the following words: Well done **MY** child go into **MY** kingdom.

BIBLE References:

2 Cor 5:10

Rom 14:8-10

Rev 20:14

1 Cor 3:10

1 Cor 3:13

1 Cor 4:5

Mat 16:27

Rev 22:12

Mat 24:

Rev 7:

Notes:

Chapter 8
White throne judgement of GOD

Our full attention is on **GOD'S** *white throne judgement as written in Rev 20:12 "And I saw the dead, small and great, standing before God, and books were opened. And another book was opened, which is the Book of Life. And the dead were judged according to their works, by the things which were written in the books. The sea gave up the dead who were in it, and Death and Hades delivered up the dead who were in them. And they were judged, each one according to his works. Then Death and Hades were cast into the lake of fire. This is the second death. And anyone not found written in the Book of Life was cast into the lake of fire." This is the final judgement. We know the first judgement was for the religious and this judgement is for the unbeliever, devil and his followers, those who died without* **GOD**. *They have died with no eternal love and life with* **GOD**.

The judgement will be fatal as the **BIBLE** said: *"standing before God"* At this white throne stood all who ran away from **GOD**, small and big, and they couldn't find any place in the whole universe and neither could they hide from **GOD**. They had to face **GOD**. I want to start by mentioning how the **BIBLE** was written. In the olden days the **BIBLE** was a continuous writing on a scroll and didn't have headings, neither chapter numbers nor verses. It was only changed in the 12th century to make it easier to track text and look up text in the **BIBLE**. The main reason I am mentioning this, is when we start reading the **BIBLE** many people try to emphasize on just one verse, and you should read verses before and after to see the verse in context to what the writer wrote when the **WORD** was given. The occurrence of false teaching is always been a fact that people takes a single verse and try to convince somebody to act just to the specific words in one verse.

My suggestion is to always try to start reading before and after the specific important verse you want to study. If you can read and understand more than one language it is also a great idea to parallel read your study.

You will then also find the older the **BIBLE** the less contradiction. Don't be a fool and try to contradict **GOD'S WORD**, be a believer of **GOD'S WORD through** the **HOLY SPIRIT** opening the channel between your minds to **GOD**.

By illustration the previous verses gives us good information, like verse 7 says: The thousand years of peace is now completed. Satan brought out of the bottomless prison and loosens to misleads the nations. The Greek "abusos" his time to mislead the time of gog and magog the battle. Then in verse 10 "*The devil. Who deceived them, was cast into the lake of fire and brimstone where the beast and the false prophet are.*" Going back to Rev 19:20 "*Then the beast was captured, and with him the false prophet who worked signs in his presence, by which he deceived those who received the mark of the beast and those who worshiped his image. These two were cast alive into the lake of fire burning with brimstone.*" SO after the 1000 years of peace he is gathering all to make war against **GOD**. But immediately after that he gets casted away to the pull of fire forever. What we also realise is that the pool of fire didn't burn them out to dust and forgotten, they will return back to the pool of fire to be punished and burn forever.

The **BIBLE** says they are still there. Only when the devil himself will be judged and thrown in the pool of fire. Immediately thereafter John says in the **BIBLE** "*I have seen a large white throne*" The moment the devil will be removed from the earthly play forever, then the white throne judgement will come to justice and its full rights. At the white throne judgement will not only be the fallen angles who sinned, thrown in the doomed pool of fire, we read in 2 Pet 2:4 "*For if God did not spare the angels who sinned, but cast them down to hell and delivered them into chains of darkness, to be reserved for judgment;*"

So the fallen angles bound in "Tartarus" will be casted in the pool of fire with the devil. Remember we are not talking about lucifer and the other angles who sinned with him. **GOD** spared those fallen angels and chained them in Tartarus; we know the word hell is not correctly translated.

The Greek word is Tartaris. Now the angels are kept in this special prison for this final judgement. We read in Jud 1:6 *"And the angels who did not keep their proper domain, but left their own abode, He has reserved in everlasting chains under darkness for the judgment of the great day;"* What I want you to know is not only human beings, but angels will appear at the white throne. Only the last couple of verses in Rev 20 explain of this great white throne, the books will be opened to see if the appeaser's names are written in this book, and then the pool of fire. This throne is huge and majestic compared to the other thrones. Also what John seen before, another lead out of this text if one could summarise it in a simple manner, is as following: Firstly we look at all the attendees, the Godless people, we read in verse 13 they are judged according to their works, everyone judged through their own works. The **BIBLE** puts it like this in verse 11 *"Then I saw a great white throne and Him who sat on it, from whose face the earth and the heaven fled away. And there was found no place for them."*

And now the books written about their life will be opened, be assured many will come from out the realm of death. In verse 13 " *"Then I saw a great white throne and Him who sat on it, from whose face the earth and the heaven fled away. And there was found no place for them. The sea gave up the dead who were in it, and Death and Hades delivered up the dead who were in them. And they were judged, each one according to his works."* We know the people in the realm of death now, are the lost. Like the story of the rich man and Lazarus explained.

The people who died without **GOD** in the realm of death will all be released that day for the judgement and brought before the white throne. These people appearing in front of **GOD** are human beings, and the fact they were in the realm of death, already knows they are sentenced. Now **GOD** will give them an opportunity when **HE** talks and shows them what their life looked like, and say the last words and in verse 7 we read *"Now when the thousand years expired, satan will be released from his prison"* and then we read how he gets casted in the pool of fire.

So chronological in **GOD'S** clock of end time happenings, this day, and we can tell now when it is, the **BIBLE** is very definite about it, and we know the church is preparing himself now.

The " Iklusia" the chosen, the children of **GOD**. After the rapture happened and the church of **JESUS CHRIST** departed to heaven. Then we know the huge seven years of depression, exclusively happenings around Israel and their purification. Dan 9 and Mat 4 explain it clearly. When the seven years are completed, **JESUS** will come visible and standing on top of mount Olive and bring the slaughter of Armageddon to an end. That will happen in the valley of Josephat. This is the old traditional "Armageddon" war grounds of Israel. It is to the north of Israel.

When this visual return of **CHRIST** happens, the following will be the start of the thousand years of peace. Then at the end of the thousand years that is when satan will be casted in the pool of fire, after his judgement at the white throne. All the people over all centuries, from Adam and Eve up to that specific moment, all the lost who died will appear before the white throne. It is a fact, right on the end of the thousand years of peace. The place for the lost without **GOD** is before **GOD'S** white throne judgement, as well as the fallen angles, will appear before this white throne. The basics of this judgement are as follows: If you study this text carefully, then we know throughout the **New Testament**, if you allow me to assemble it, the ground where **GOD** will judge humans.

Firstly the **BIBLE** is very definite about this section in Rev 20 that the death was judged "books *were opened, which is the book of life.*" The book of their works was opened, the heavenly record of the sinner's works and wrong words, wrong doings of individuals. **JESUS** was very clear and specific on that when HE explained in Mat 12:36&37 *"But I say to you that for every idle word men may speak, they will give account of it in the Day of Judgment. For by your words you will be justified, and by your words you will be condemned."* We can definitely see all our words we spoke on earth will be revealed that judgement day.

That is what **JESUS** said: *"every idle word men may speak, they will give account of it in the Day of Judgment"* The books of their works and we know it the people who died without **CHRIST** in their life, and remember the believers will not be at this judgement, just the non religious.

They have to give account for every idle word they spoke. Their deeds and their words. It gives us a bit of peace of mind to know that these wrong doers will be judged for all the wrong they have done and also treated not guilty people badly and as well as the cruel deed they have done to people. They die without the **LORD** and said these bad things, with or without the judgement chair in every country; despite if they get away lightly, despite they leave early of their sentenced period and despite the unfairness in our legal judgement system. There is one judgement chair they will never escape from, and that is the white throne judgement of **GOD**.

Everybody will appear before the living **GOD**, and need to answer for before **GOD** of all his or her wrong doing, on that huge day, and it won't be in front of an unfair judge, but in front of **GOD** with no mercy. The sinner has to know this, I need to tell you: your day will come when you stand before **GOD** when you die without **GOD**. Because when you die without **GOD**, you die in sin, and if you die in sin you are definitely lost, and if you die as lost you will appear at the white throne judgement chair.

At this chair you will be punished by the **CREATOR, GOD** who will have no mercy on you, no more chances, any more feeling sorry for, just the final judgement.

The second aspect of this base judgement is the law of your conscious, but there are people who said some people never had **GOD'S WORD** to read or never heard of it. Now how will **GOD** judge them? My answer is clear and definite when we read the **BIBLE** we read in Rom 2:12 giving us no excuse *"For as many as have sinned without law will also perish without law, and as many as have sinned in the law will be judged by the law"* Now we have two laws. The one law; the law which judges your works, and then there is something else, how do they get judged without the law? Let's read further: 13 *"(for not the hearers of the law are just in the sight of God, but the doers of the law will be justified; for when Gentiles, who do not have the law, by nature do the things in the law, these, although not having the law, are a law to themselves, who show the work of the law written in their hearts, their conscience also bearing witness, and between themselves their thoughts accusing or else excusing them)"* what's going to happen is there is a judgement of conscious, the law of conscious.

Then **GOD** will judge you according to your conscious. Isn't it what the **WORD** says? Your conscious are always telling you when you do something bad. Even if you don't have a **BIBLE** or a law book, and even if no one tells you about your wrong doing, you know in your heart of hearts wrong from right. Then we have the Law of Moses through this sell, the complete **OLD TESTAMENT** from Genesis up to Malachi, all the books of the **OLD TESTAMENT**, all 39 books will be the basis. Everybody who knows the **BIBLE** and now also the **NEW TESTAMENT**, the full gospel and will be judged according to the gospels. Rom 2:16 *"in the day when God will judge the secrets of men by Jesus Christ, according to my gospel."*

Paul is very specific about this judgement. **GOD** is going to judge the non believer according to Mathew, Mark, Luke, John and the complete **New Testament.**

Those 27 books, in other words all you have read so far, and everything you have heard. The Gospel the **NEW TESTAMENT** is the measurement, the law book of Moses the **OLD TESTAMENT** is the measurement, both and your conscious and as well as the writing of your personnel deeds in the books of life, every wrong doing in life, every wrong thinking, every wrong thing you spoke in your life. All these things will serve, and the **BIBLE** totally summarises it in Joh 12:48 *"He who rejects me, and does not receive my words, has that which judges him— the word that I have spoken will judge him in the last day."* Listen very carefully: **JESUS** puts it clearly, **HE** does not want to judge you, and you have another opportunity while you are still alive, to confess your sins. To seek **HIS** forgiveness and to get to become **HIS** child. But after you die, will every word you heard in your life about the **WORD** of **GOD** count against you at the white throne judgement. In the last day of the final judgement of **GOD**. The base of the judgement is this: And I want to say this on this level: Rev 20:15 *"And anyone not found written in the Book of Life was cast into the lake of fire."* You will be casted in the pool of fire. How definite and final is that?

The book of life opened, we have read in verse 12 *"and books were opened. And another book was opened, which is the Book of Life. And the dead were judged according to their works, by the things which were written in the books."* When that book opened and your name does not appear in it, you will burn in hell forever. What's going to happen that day is **GOD** will ask an angel: look and see if his name appears there? His answer will be: *no it is not written in here!* They who stood in front of the white throne judgement, who came out of the realm of death, is attending specifically there because the name omits from the book of life.

And the final test is going to be the test of your conscious, the test of Moses, the test of the gospel after the test of your own record and wrong doing, thoughts and wrong words. After the witness of the **WORD** of **GOD**.

The final test is so clear and reads finally: *"when some bodies name is not there"* no wonder **JESUS** said to **HIS** disciples in Luk 10:12 in so many words. HE said" *be glad that your names are written in the book of life."* If there is something you need to thank **GOD** for the rest of your life, when you know your name is written in the book of life. Because when your name is omited the day of the white throne judgement, the final reason why you will be casted in the pool of fire. The Judge will be **GOD** the **FATHER**, in verse 12 *"I saw them standing in front of GOD"* and with **GOD** the **LORD JESUS CHRIST**. Because in Joh 5:27 **JESUS** said: HIS **FATHER** gives **HIM** the power to judge that day and **JESUS** said: *"But Jesus answered them, "My Father has been working until now, and I have been working." and has given Him authority to execute judgment also, because He is the Son of Man."* On your right-hand is going to be **GOD**, and on **HIS** side **GOD JESUS** the **SON**.

The aim of this judgement is to bring all non believers to the white throne. The quilty will hear their ruling formally. His punishment forever: the pool of fire. The resultant of the white throne judgement will be: All being judge then will go into the pool of fire for eternity.

The fact that it is a white throne is the sign of purity, safety, and of holiness, and honesty, and fairness. Everything is transparent, with no favouritism the one before the other, it means all equal. Nobody would say **GOD** treated them unfairly, **GOD'S** judgement is always honest. We have to separate this white throne from the 1000 years that happened before that, at the "Bhma" the judgement seat, the throne. JESUS stood before the Bhma, Pilate's throne his judgement seat. But isn't it an amazing thing that here everything will be reversed. Now Pilate will stand before the judgment throne of **CHRIST**. How do you think he will feel on that day when he treated **CHRIST** as though **HE** was nothing? He used **CHRIST** to barter with Herod. He pawned around **CHRIST** as though he were nothing and now Pilate will stand before **CHRIST**. Where the children of **GOD** appears to receive their crowns. Think how awful it will be at the white thrown judgement when you hear the words JESUS spoke about the fallen angles and all sinners: Mat 25:41 *"Then He will also say to those on the left hand, 'Depart from Me, you cursed, into the everlasting fire prepared for the devil and his angels."*

That will be the last words of **GOD** that the non religious will hear for eternity. My blood clots in my veins just thinking about this. But a fact is, people dying without **GOD**, are lost without **GOD** and dies as a sinner. All will hear those words with all the fallen angles. *"Depart from Me, you cursed, into the everlasting fire prepared for the devil and his angels:"* Prepared for the devil and those angels. This will be the end of godless, and in the hell you will never stop burning. The **BIBLE** says in Rev 14:11 *"And the smoke of their torment ascends forever and ever; and they have no rest day or night, who worship the beast and his image, and whoever receives the mark of his name."* There will be no rest.

Don't you think it is by far better for you to reach out to **GOD** and get **HIM** on your side? If you are not sure that your name is in the book of life, do not hesitate, pray to **GOD** through **JESUS** to make sure your name is written in the book of life. Ask **GOD** to give the **HOLY SPIRIT** an opportunity to guide you in truth and right ways to be serious on your way forward with your relationship with **GOD** and you working for **HIM**. After all **GOD** created us to make disciples for **HIM** and praise and honour **HIM** always.

Live after Death

BIBLE References:

Rev 20:12
Rev 19:20
2 Pet 2:4
Jud 1:6
Rev 20:7, 11 & 13
Dan 9
Mat 24
Mat 12:36&37
Rom 2:16
Joh 12:48
Rev 20:15
Luk 10:12
Joh 5:17
Mat 25:41
Rev 14:11

Notes:

Chapter 9
Glory of the new earth

Who doesn't want to know what the new earth is about? In Rev 21:1 to 8 *"Now I saw a new heaven and a new earth, for the first heaven and the first earth had passed away. 2 Also there was no more sea. Then I, John, saw the holy city, New Jerusalem, coming down out of heaven from God, prepared as a bride adorned for her husband. 3 And I heard a loud voice from heaven saying, "Behold, the tabernacle of God is with men, and He will dwell with them, and they shall be His people. God Himself will be with them and be their God. 4 And God will wipe away every tear from their eyes; there shall be no more death, nor sorrow, nor crying. There shall be no more pain, for the former things have passed away. 5 Then He who sat on the throne said, "Behold, I make all things new." And He said to me, "Write, for these words are true and faithful. 6 And He said to me, "It is done! I am the Alpha and the Omega, the Beginning and the End. I will give of the fountain of the water of life freely to him who thirsts. 7 He who overcomes shall inherit all things, and I will be his God and he shall be My son. 8 But the cowardly, unbelieving, abominable, murderers, sexually immoral, sorcerers, idolaters, and all liars shall have their part in the lake which burns with fire and brimstone, which is the second death."*

Behind the spiritual curtain of life, we might as well look into what's there after life and death. Our focus is to zoom in and have a peep in life after death, and after resurrection. Rev 20:6 *"Blessed and holy is he who has part in the first resurrection. Over such the second death has no power, but they shall be priests of God and of Christ, and shall reign with Him a thousand years."* To be part of the first resurrection and receive a glorified body. As we read in 1Joh 3:2

"Beloved, now we are children of God; and it has not yet been revealed what we shall be, but we know that when He is revealed, we shall be like Him, for we shall see Him as He is."

We receive exactly the same glorified body like **JESUS**. In Rev 20:6 it was confirmed. This chapter starts with: *"Now I saw a new heaven"* exactly what we just read. *"and a new earth"* Then John tells us this wonderful thing he saw. We also know that **GOD** sort off transported him into the future to that day to give him a clear vision of what he needs to write down. This is then a prophetical word. Remember what this word in Revelations says: Rev 1:3 *"Blessed is he who reads and those who hear the words of this prophecy, and keep those things which are written in it; for the time is near."* Clearly what's written there is a prophecy and whoever hears or reads this and keeps those things, now remember we have read and heard it loud and clear.

Let us look into this prophesy and take a glimpse at this wonderful holy advantage of this prophesy expressed in Revelation. The new heaven and new earth is a new type of society. There will be a new city, there is a new light, there is a new society a lifestyle which John saw when the **LORD** gave him a glimpse of the new prepared earth. It is these new things he glanced at. Which gives him the full picture to write in precise words what he visualises? We also realise Revelation is the last book in the **BIBLE**. Also warned in Rev 22 to never add or take away what's written in **GOD'S WORD**, but there is a definite similarity and parallel in relation with Genesis when **GOD** wrote of the beginning of earth.

The Genesis story, the creation story, especially the first three chapters and also the last three chapters parallel with the book Revelation. It is actually a fantastic combination melted together. We start with the beginning of the **BIBLE** the creation of the human being and the rest were created and all progressed around that.

Then we go to the end of the **BIBLE** the last chapter and many answers were given and a parallel line was drawn between Genesis and Revelation. It is from the start of the **BIBLE** write to the end of the **BIBLE**. This is a wonderful unit and combination of facts. All answers on what happened on earth in Genesis and the last book Revelation, where **GOD** determined how the humans will live on earth. **HE** created a new society.

Let me show you what I mean with a definitive similarity in life after death, after the resurrection of the righteous. Remember the question is, and don't overlook it. The question we need to answer is: what does life look like after death? What happened from the resurrection of the believer?

It brings it to the new order where the child of **GOD** has a glorified body. The resurrected glorified body equal to **JESUS'S** body **HE** received. We know it was **GOD'S** purpose to give all his children the same body as in Rom 8. What does the new order look like where we going to and in front of our eyes all the answers? When we compare it with Genesis it is a fantastic revelation **GOD** mentions here. As example against the first word in the **BIBLE**. How the **BIBLE** does starts? Gen 1:1 *"In the beginning GOD created heaven and earth"* and now interesting Rev 21 John starts with these words: *"I saw a new heaven and a new earth"* See the parallel line? Then in Gen 1:10 the sea was created as separation, and in Rev 21:1 we read: *"Also there was no more sea"* no more sea like in Genesis 1. But there is something very interesting I am not explaining now. Will mention though in Gen 1:5 *"God called the light Day, and the darkness He called Night."* In Rev 21:5 we read *"Then He who sat on the throne said, "Behold, I make all things new."* And when **GOD** renews all, we read in verse 23 the city does not need the sun and moon for light, **GOD HIMSELF** was the light. There will never be darkness. All lovely and light in this heavenly city. Then we also read in Gen 1:16 about the sun and moon supplying light to the earth. The sun for the daylight and the moon for the night light. Then we read in Rev 21:4 *"GOD will wipe away every tear from their eyes"* can you observe all these new changes?

Yes we read **GOD** makes all new. The death we read in Gen 2:17 changed to *"there shall be no more death"* with this we have a promise, no more death. The curse of Gen 3:17 what **GOD** has put on earth, because of the fall of men, will be taken away forever. In Rev 22:3 *"And there shall be no more curse"*. You can clearly see what happened in the Old Testament in the Garden of Eden and now declared all gone. When we read in Rev 21:4 *"**GOD** will wipe away every tear from their eyes"*. There will be no more sadness and trouble. The **LORD** places us in a total new order.

The previous taken away totally. Satan revealed in Gen 3:1 the snake, called the devil, satan. In Rev 22:2 there will be a new road either side of the river and trees with fruit the **BIBLE** says, all totally new. Interesting just before we read in Rev 20:10 *"The devil, who deceived them, was cast into the lake of fire"* We can clearly see satan came onto the earthly roll and tempted all human and trampled humanity, will not be in the new earth but thrown in the pool of fire forever. Then the tree of live **GOD** forbids eating from after the fall of men. The humans were not allow to enter or eat of the tree and **GOD** puts a Cherubim at the entrance with a flaming sword which turned every way, to keep the way of the tree of life. We read in the new order **GOD'S** children on the new earth are free to eat off the tree of life.

It is written word for word from verse 1 *"And he showed me a pure river of water of life, clear as crystal, proceeding from the throne of God and of the Lamb. In the middle of its street, and on either side of the river, was the tree of life, which bore twelve fruits, each tree yielding its fruit every month. The leaves of the tree were for the healing of the nations."* People get invited to eat from this tree. JESUS HIMSELF says in Rev 22:14 *"Blessed are those who do His commandments, that they may have the right to the tree of life, and may enter through the gates into the city."* The tree that was forbidden is now opened to eat from for all **GOD'S** children.

The humans chased away by **GOD** in Gen 3:23 where **GOD** removed them from Eden, where **GOD** came to visit them in the evening breeze. Is absolutely welcome now to visit, now in Rev 20:3 and 4 with no restriction.

The thrones of **GOD** and **JESUS** will be there. **HIS** servants will serve **HIM**. They will see his face. **HIS** name will be on their foreheads. No more night. They don't need sunlight or any lamp, **GOD HIMSELF** will be the light. The prehistoric human dwelling at the earthly river in Gen 2:10 where we read of the river flowing from out the garden and when we read about these rivers starting from the garden. We read now in Rev 20:1 *"and he showed me a pure river of water of life, clear as crystal, proceding from the throne of GOD and the LAMB."*

You see now the parallel line from what counted against the human beings the sin of men taken away. A New order. It is wonderful to see what **GOD** saved for us in the glories and everlasting future. This forces me to ask the following question: Is it true that this city where all this will take place with this uncountable will be my inheritance?

This new city of **GOD** is for all **HIS** children and they will live there forever as we read in Rev 21:2 *"Then I, John, saw the holy city, New Jerusalem, coming down of heaven from GOD, prepared as a bride adorned for her husband."* It is just our heavenly **FATHER** who creates the outmost beautiful things, only the best; **HE** is the only living **GOD** who creates the unbelievable beauty. And to take it further it comes down out of the heaven onto the earth. It is called the heavenly Jerusalem. In Heb 12:23 *"heavenly Jerusalem"* and in Rev 3:12 *"heavenly Jerusalem"* In Rev 21:2 the bride of **GOD** because she is now prepared like a bride adorned for her husband. Interesting that **GOD** calls it like that because the saved, the children of **GOD**, is the bride of **GOD**. We will live in the city forever. Then in Rev 21:10 the city is called the **HOLY Jerusalem**. So we have the heavenly Jerusalem, the bride of **GOD**, the **HOLY Jerusalem**, because it is holy and never again will enter the unholy, not clean, no lies, ugliness, never again. There will be no crook, no thieve, no deceiver, no murderer can enter the city. It will never happen again.

The **BIBLE** is very clear about this in Rev 21:27 *"But there shall by no means enter it anything that defiles, or causes an abomination or a lie, but only those who are written in the Lamb's Book of Life."* Isn't that fantastic, only the righteous of **GOD**. It is called the **HOLY CITY** because only the holy are allowed to be part of this holy city. Also a wonderful discovery as we read through Rev 21 and even in Rev 22 we see **GOD'S** holy number twelve. There are twelve specific promises, blessings revealed in the new order on the new earth. Where the new earth descent from heaven. In the life after death, as child of **GOD** these blessings become mine. The saved will live there. Also read Rev 21:3 *"GOD HIMSELF will be with them and be their GOD."* **GOD** forever be with the human being. **GOD** comes to live with us. On the new earth, in the **NEW JERUSALEM**, the throne and the **LAMB** in Rev 22:3

GOD'S throne will be on earth. Inside the **NEW JERUSALEM**. Read the complete Rev 21 & 22 it states it clearly. It is definitely a blessing to have **GOD** with you forever.

Nothing will separate us from **GOD** again and we will be with **HIM** forever and **HE** will be a **GOD** for us. More than just a spiritual experience, **HE** will be there in person. We will be **HIS** nation and **HIS** children forever, remember without HIM nothing exists. Nothing will separate is from **HIS** love and from **HIS SON JESUS CHRIST**. The saved and **GOD** lives in the city together in the Holy City. We read in the **BIBLE GOD** will wipe our tears; **HE** will literally wipe our tears. As from the beginning of earth when the first sin was committed the human beings are suffering. We cannot stop brokenness the **BIBLE** says in Ps 126 *"Those who sow in tears shall reap in joy."*

In the new order are tears something of the past, no more suffering as we know it by hard in our life today, will never happen forever and eternity. The **BIBLE** tells us further, another blessing; there will be no more death. The sting of death named sin will be no more, and casted in the pool of fire forever. Rev 20 and 21 says it clearly that the dead will be thrown in the pool of fire. If there is no more death there will be no more sin.

The devil and his evil won't be there anymore, everything unholy gone in the pool of fire. What a blessing of no more dying.

There will be no more sorrow. In Rev 21 says no more sadness, and no more weeping. Two more blessings, no more sadness and weeping, and come to think of that how sad we as humans can get when someone dies. These things will be gone forever. The next blessing we read off is no more pain as we acknowledge it on earth. What a blessed promise, because we have a new order where we will not get tired as we are getting now.

You will have every second this full cup of energy running over of joy. Even the tree of live will reproduce and you will fill yourself with life and drink of the living water flowing from the throne. You will never get thirsty, for water and the flowing love from **GOD'S** living water.

You will definitely be filled with joy and happiness and will have no needs accept to praise **GOD**. He who is in **GOD** will inherit everything and will be a winner. In Rev 21:7 *"He who overcomes shall inherit all things and I will be his GOD and he shall be MY son."*

What a fantastic promise that we will inherit all and that there will be no trespassing from the evil and no liars and thieves steeling from us, because everything in the **NEW JERUSALEM** belongs to all. And the fixed promise *"And I will be your GOD"* and I will be his son. Look at this heavenly relationship with **GOD** the **FATHER** and the **SON**. This is what **GOD** has for you if you could start and hold on these promises and have a holy life for **HIM** now.

BIBLE References:

Rev 21:1	Rev 20:6		
1 Joh	Rev 20:6		
Rev 1:3	Rom 8		
Gen 1:1	Gen 1:10	Rev 21:1	
Gen 1:5	Rev 21:5		
Gen 1:16	Rev 21:4		
Gen 2:17			
Gen 3:17	Rev 22:3		
Gen 3:16	Rev 21:4		
Gen 3:1	Rev 22:2	Rev 20:10	
Gen 3:23	Rev 20:3&4		
Gen 2:10	Rev 20:1		
Heb 12:23			
Rev 3:12	Rev 21:2	Rev 21:10	Rev 21:27	Rev 21:3
Rev 22:3			
Ps 126			
Rev 21:7			

Notes:

Chapter 10
The new Jerusalem – the new GOD CITY

Let us look at the new **GOD CITY.** *Wonderful new things await us in this new* **CITY.** *To start I just want to mention when we read Revelation you will read* **seven things.** *The first in Rev 2:17 "And I will give him a white stone, and on the stone a new name written which no one knows except him who receives it."* **GOD** *will give* **HIS** *child a* **new name** *for eternity. This name describes who you really are and your character and your personal insides. Your personality.* **GOD** *knows you and gives you a specific name. You see a new name for the perseverance. Then in Rev 3:12 a* **new name for CHRIST. JESUS** *will also receive a new name for eternity when* **GOD** *places the new earth on earth. We will all know* **HIS NAME.** *Then in Rev 3:12 the* **New Jerusalem.** *You as a child of* **GOD,** *believer in* **JESUS** *will get* **access** *to the* **NEW JERUSALEM.**

This is the new **GOD CITY**, and then in Rev 5:9 the fourth new thing, the **new song.** We will sing a new song in heaven to the

FATHER and the SON'S honour. And we also read in Rev 21 about the new heaven. GOD is going to set the new heaven and in Rev 21:1 the sixth thing in the second part of the text, the "New Earth" The last thing in Rev 21:5 *"All new things"* GOD said it clearly. "And HE who was seated on the throne said, behold, I am making all things new. Also HE said; "write this down, for these words is thruthworthy and true." Thus the wonder of life after death for us in CHRIST knows we go into a new life, a new order, in a new GOD city a complete new situation. Away from the devil, away from sin, away of the earthly struggle. Away from all evil and ugliness and go into the glory of GOD.

Then the focus shifts to Rev 21 a total new order. This is for the believer in place, and what the unbeliever face in verse 8 is clear on that.

"But for the cowardly, the faithless, the detestable, as for murderers, sexually immoral, corcerers, idolaters, and all liars, their portion will be in the lake that burns with fire and sulphur, which is the second death." Here you see eight groups of people who go to the pool of fire, hell forever.

Also why they go to hell. It is those dying without GOD. The frightened, the fainthearted. It is them who's afraid of humans, but not afraid of GOD and not lived a GODLY life. Then the second group the unbelievers the ones who died without faith in GOD. This is actually all categories of the bad of the human race. The horrible, the gene infected with natural lustfulness, like homosexualism, bestiality and murderers. They who shed innocent blood.

The sexual immoral, and very interesting the Greek text "darnois" "pornografia" is actually the word where we got the word pornography from, the word for men and woman prostitutes. And magician which is not a good translated word, and in Greek it is "farmakeio" a reference of "pharmacy" drugs, it refers to a place where you purchase medicine. A reference to drugs. They who are drug addicted, and servants or worshipers of idols, and they who picked things above **GOD**, an idol. Then the eighth group the liar. The hell is the place for the liar forever. The father of all lies is the devil. Joh 8:44 *"You are of your father the devil, and your will is to do your father's desires. He was a murderer from the beginning, and does not stand in the truth, because there is no truth in him."* So somebody who lies, and love to talk lies, and practice lies have the devil as father, but are against **GOD** and therefore a enemy of **GOD**.

In Rev 22:15 another two additional aspects are named. We read about the dogs, and the same time we read the ones who love lies and who does lies. But outside the **GOD CITY** is what Rev 20:15 refers to, in the **GOD CITY** will only be **HIS** children, but outside lives the dogs, the murderers, sexually immoral, sorcerers, idolaters, and all liars. You see here is mentioned two extras "the dogs" dogs is the reference to humans who are used to living in their own impurity, where the dog is a good example of impurity.

Like in 2 Pet 2:22 *"It has happened unto them according to the true proverb, the dog turning to his own vomit again, and the saw that had washed to wallowing in the mire. "* The false prophets are also falls under this metaphor of dogs. Phil 3:2 *"Beware of the dogs, beware of the evil workers, beware of concision."* The context of use of these words "dogs" by Paul referred to false prophets.

GOD'S place for them is the pool of fire, and then we read of the new things which actually make up a group of people. Everybody who love lies. Many people are using lies as an instrument of own ungodliness. We see that in the last two chapters of the **BIBLE**.

There is an absolute division between the children of **GOD** and the children of the devil. Those who love righteousness and exercise it, those who love lies and unrighteousness, and died in that state. When we look at the **GOLD CITY** and we read **JESUS** saying in Rev 21:9 *"Come, I will show you the BRIDE, the wife of the LAMB. And he carried me away in the SPIRIT to a great, high mountain, and showed me the holy city Jerusalem coming down out of heaven from GOD"* I have to tell you this city exist already, when we read in Heb 12:21 this **GOD CITY** exist already and Moses said I am troubled and shudder in verse 22 *"Indeed so terrifying was the sight that Moses said. I tremble with fear. But you have come to Mount Zion and to the city of the living GOD, the Heavenly Jerusalem, and to innumerable angels in festal gathering, and to the assembly of the firstborn who are enrolled in heaven, and to GOD, the JUDGE of all, and* *to the spirits of the righteous made perfect, and to JESUS, the MEDIATOR of the new covenant"*

You can clearly see through the blood of JESUS the spirits of the righteous arrive at the JUDGE of all, at GOD of the congregation of the first borne who are enrolled in heaven. This festival gathering with us in the heavenly Jerusalem. Those who departed before us, the believers who died before us, they are already in the GOLDCITY because the BIBLE says: *"and to the spirits of the righteous made perfect,"* This city the BIBLE talks about which comes down to earth from GOD is already there, exist already.

It is located in the highest heaven where GOD lives and will descents on the specific moment when GOD wants it there, we read in Rev 21:1 *"Then I saw a new heaven and a new earth, for the first heaven and the first earth had passed away, and the sea was no more."* It is something in the past. Now onto the new earth descents, the New Jerusalem, the CITY of GOD onto the earth. A massive big CITY and the BIBLE describes it clearly as a cube form in Rev 21:16 *"The city lies foursquare, its length the same as its width.*

And he measured the city with his rod, 12,000 stadia. Its length and width and height are equal." In other words the city's form is a cube form. Its height, length and width are equal. If you want to know how big this GOD CITY is: Converted in miles it is 1500 mile and 2400 km in our measurement. We have this CITY towering high above as the NEW JERUSALEM. This new GOD CITY descents from heaven onto earth.

The new Jerusalem – the new GOD CITY | 155

We also know that **GOD** is placing the **CITY** where Jerusalem is at the moment, interesting we read in Rev 21:1 *"Also there was no more sea."* If we take a cube of 2400km and put it centrally on today's Jerusalem it will cover most of the Mediterranean Sea. No wonder the **BIBLE** says there was no more sea. Not to say that the sea around the earth wouldn't exist anymore. But the Mediterranean Sea as we know it now, and in the **BIBLE** period was the sea against Israel coast. The larger part of that sea can't exist anymore. In regards to this **CITY** descending from heaven and the changes as described the new earth **GOD** will transform to fit the new **CITY** on earth. Also very valuable that **GOD** guards the **CITY** with a high wall. The wall will be 300 foot, 100 meter high wall around the **CITY**. Every side has three gates and each entrance is completely cut of a pearl. This **CITY** is definitely a city where **GOD** will rule.

Because **12** is the sign of **GOD'S** Government properties. When you look at the earth for example and heavens around earth, then you get the **12** star figures, the sign of the zodiac and that is divided into **12** sections.

All around us visible. As you realise **GOD** rules out of the heavens on earth. When you look at the new earth, in Rev 12:21 there are **12** gates and **12** angles at each entrance and then we read about the **12** gate names according to the BIBLE'S traditionally **12** tribes of Israel, and these names will be written on each gate. Then we read in verse 14 that this **CITY** will have **12** foundations and on it will be written the names of the **12** Apostles of the **LAMB**. We also read about the height of the wall is **12 x 12** in verse 17 *"Then he measured its wall: one hundred and fourty four cubits"* That is **12 x 12**. We read there are **12** precious stones. Let us read verses 19 and 20

"The foundations of the wall of the city were adorned with all kinds of precious stones: the first foundation was jasper, the second sapphire, the third chalcedony, the fourth emerald, the fifth sardonyx, the sixth sardius, the seventh chrysolite, the eighth beryl, the ninth topaz, the tenth chrysoprase, the eleventh jacinth, and the twelfth amethyst." What is this telling you? It tells you that this **GOD CITY** rules by itself.

You have to remember there were **12** elders, **12** tribes of Israel, **12** Apostles. That is why **GOD** showed us through **CHRIST** **HE** picked **12** Apostles in the **NEW TESTAMENT**. In the **OLD TESTAMENT** there were **12** Tribes of Israel. You can see **12** is a huge figure in the **BIBLE**, you see the **12** comes up many times. The figure of **GOD'S** Government. The indication of this **NEW GOD CITY** where we go to as children of **GOD**, the **CITY** where **GOD** rules. There are no different dictators in the world that you see with their own special agendas, Butism and all of these things that we disgust in this world, which we must bear in this earthly order. When we enter this new **GOD CITY**, it is a theocratic government. Then we know that **GOD** rules, and **GOD** rules all Jerusalem that descended from heaven over earth. And it will be a precious government with a righteous **GOD** with a **HOLY GOD** it is my pleasure to know that this is the place we are heading for in the new order. Surely the **LORD** says the streets of this **GOD CITY** are of pure gold.

And the BIBLE says *"The city had no need of the sun or of the moon to shine in it, for the glory of God illuminated it. The Lamb is its light.* "And the LAMB is the lamp. GOD'S visual presence in the CITY shines throughout this CITY.

The sun's rays cannot even shine over this city. For the glory of GOD, GOD made the sun but GOD HIMSELF, which is so much greater and more glorious than the sun, the sun is only part of GOD'S creation.

But GOD HIMSELF who is the CREATOR and the glory and light of the city lives, is so great that the sun and moon are not necessary to relieve it by day and by itself. And then we read that only the nations of those saved in verse 23 are in the light of it. There must be something in the light. There must be something like pure crystal clear.

This light must be special and it must be very precious to just walk in the light and the BIBLE says in verse 24: *"And the nations of those who are saved shall walk in its light, and the kings of the earth bring their glory and honour into it."* And it's not because night no longer exists in the universe, because the seasons are continuing, the years, many are continuing. Although we are in this order, but the fact that GOD lives there will shine HIS light out of darkness, the BIBLE says in verse 25: *"Its gates shall not be shut at all by day (there shall be no night there)."* And the people entering those gates will become aware of the glory and honour of the nations. Now you have to pay attention to verse 27 *"Its gates shall not be shut at all by day (there shall be no night there). But there shall by no means enter it anything that defiles, or causes an abomination or a lie, but only those who are written in the Lamb's Book of Life."* If your name is missing in the book of life, you cannot access that city. Only if your name is written in the **BOOK** of **LIFE**.

That's why it's so important in the last chapter, it's just the next chapter, we read where **JESUS** says in Rev 22:13 to 15 *"I am the Alpha and the Omega, the Beginning and the End, the First and the Last.*

Blessed are those who do HIS commandments that they may have the right to the tree of life, and may enter through the gates into the city. But outside are dogs and sorcerers and sexually immoral and murderers and idolaters, and whoever loves and practices a lie." But outside is all the Godless as you read in verse 15 and then the call in verse 17. *"And the Spirit and the bride say, "Come!" And let him who hears say, "Come!" And let him who thirsts come. Whoever desires let him take the water of life freely."*

Can you believe **GOD** offers you the city for free, **JESUS** tells you in Joh 14:3 *"And if I go and prepare a place for you, I will come again and receive you to Myself; that where I am, there you may be also."* **GOD** presents to you the glory of **GOD**. The glory of this **GOD CITY** the glory of eternity, without rest and time forever and ever without a break, there without breaking a second, you can forever be in a rest pause and enter into peace of **GOD**. I repeat enter into the peace of **GOD**.

Enter into the glory of **GOD**, and all this for nothing. Now the question is how is this possible? This is certainly possible because **JESUS** paid the price on the cross. **HE** gave **HIS** life to make a new future for you. That you can be taken in glory from this sinful world. Yes, it costs something. That you stay in **HIM** with your faith. It costs you to confess your sins against **HIM**. But you do not have to pay for this privilege. You cannot get it. You cannot earn it. You cannot do anything about it.

All it takes is to truly accept **JESUS CHRIST** as your **Saviour**, to take **HIM** as your **SAVIOR** and your **LORD** in your life and to follow **HIM** and to serve **HIM** every day of your life. And then you move from this life, this side of death to eternity in **HIS** eternal rest. A man wrote one day, "**He who makes provision for this life alone, but not for eternity, shows for a moment but a fool forever.**" I need to remind you that death has no calendar showing you that he will not come, you do not know. Death has a key for every door. You cannot hide from him; death does not ask excuses if he fetch you. Death does not ask if you're ready. He comes to every human being. What will happen to you in life after death?

There is only one answer or in the glory of **GOD** or in hell. Make the choice now not later. Take **HIM** right now and ask **HIM** forgiveness. **HE** waits!

BIBLE References:

Rev 2:17
Rev 3:12
Rev 5:9
Rev 21:1
Rev 21:5
Joh 8:40
Rev 22:15
Rev 20:15
2 Pet 2:22
Phi 3:2
Heb 12:21

| Rev 21:1 | Rev 21:16 | Rev 12:21 |

Notes:

Chapter 11
How does a child of GOD DIE?

How does a child of GOD die in peace? We read in Ps 90 how Moses a man of **GOD** speaks to **GOD** in prayer. Also about death and things surrounding death and about life. He will for example mention in verse 10 about ages of people: *"The days of our lives are seventy years; and if by reason of strength they are eighty years, yet their boast is only labor and sorrow; for it is soon cut off, and we fly away."* How old are you? Maybe 50, 70 or 80? If you made 80 it is only the grace of GOD. The life of a human wasn't always that short. You will read in Genesis that **GOD** let the **Old Testament** people life up to just under a thousand years. That was calendar years; we are talking of 365 days per year, 24 hour cycles, and 12 hour days. That was a fact, the oldest man ever lived on earth was Metsusaleg who was 969 years old. That was close to a thousand years. And later in Genesis **GOD** shorten it to about 120 years old. You will read that in Genesis 6 and other relevant verses, **GOD** shorten the human's living years. Then **GOD** spoke to Moses and he wrote the average is 70 and for

How does a child of GOD DIE? | 163

one or other reason if you are strong you could reach 80 years old. If **GOD** *blesses us with good health and guide and beware us we can reach 80. We got to tell people older than 80 how blessed they are and that every day after a blessed gift of* **GOD** *is, with reason behind that, to tell the younger generation of the goodness of* **GOD**. *Yes I am talking about the religious, a reborn in* **GOD**, *the truthful servant of* **GOD** *our creator.*

Now a true Christian, how does such a person die? A child of **GOD** and his last fight on earth. What happens there? Our last fight with death. Do I have the assurance of the promise of **GOD** with **HIS** presence and perseverance with me? That **HE** will be next to me after I died into death. You know we read in many books with themes like:

The art how not to get old, the art to eat correctly, the art to live healthy, the art to do healthy exercises and to strengthen our bodies.

The question remains: have nobody thought of writing books of how you should die blessed? We always teach one another how to live, and from a young age our children how to have a good life. But I belief there wasn't enough said or written about how to die blessed. And the art to fold this earthly tent residence of ours up. How do I die to please **GOD**? How do I fold my earthly body to be ready?

Listen the BIBLE stipulates that clearly in 2 Cor 5:1 *"For we know that if our earthly house, this tent, is destroyed, we have a building from God, a house not made with hands, eternal in the heavens."* When we die life departs from this body to somewhere else. Life did not end yet. Life just go out of our body and moves over the dead's Jordan to another place. The question is still: what happens that moment with my body? My body turns to dust, goes back to earth. Can you remember what **GOD** said to Adam: Dust you are and will return to dust? **GOD** referred to the body not the spirit, where **GOD** blew life in Adams nostrils when Adam was created. Out of clay soil, out of dust this body laid in front of **GOD**. The BIBLE said: *"And the LORD God formed man of the dust of the ground, and breathed into his nostrils the breath of life; and man became a living being."* Now when this breath departs from the body, the body turns back to dust. The question: how do we need to fold this earthly tent, our body up whilst I know I am busy dying, how should I know how to do it?

The art of how to die. What better guidance is there besides the BIBLE? **GOD'S WORD** shows us how to die safely in **HIS** arms. We read in Amos 4:12 *"Therefore thus will I do to you, O Israel; because I will do this to you, prepare to meet your God, O Israel!"* How do you do that? Defiantly yes, we will say give your life to **JESUS**, repent your sins, take **HIM** as your personal savior and to get saved. And that **HE** is your savior of your life.

And that your name is in the **BOOK** of **LIVE**. That's all true. That is not actually the question. The question we ask is: How should I prepare to meet **GOD**. How do I die? Is the **BIBLE** not telling us how to die?

It seems that all people are just happy to climb down this earthly stage of life, with only what their own knowledge tells them. And everybody think that is enough. It is frightening to die unknowingly and surely there are better ways to die or to resurrect.

It is possible, the **BIBLE** is full about that, where we can see how to prepare at the end of our earthly road in stillness, assured everything is well. It is well with my soul. Your eyes fixed on **JESUS**, your companion, the only **JESUS** who opened the door to the **NEW JERUSALEM** and the entrance **HE** opened for you to heaven. To the paradise the glory of **GOD**. Why do our hearts have to rumble thinking of death? Why tell me why? We might as well as Simon said in the olden days in Luk 2:29 & 30 we read when **JESUS** were eight days old **HIS** earthly parents brought him to be circumcised in the temple. Simon and Anna were busy praying. Simon was an old man when he saw **JESUS** only eight days old, and took **HIM** in his arms and said the following words: This old man, a grey-haired man, do you see this picture? He took this baby in his arms, but it wasn't just any baby, this time it was **JESUS CHRIST** who became human. Who became flesh, who adapted from the **GODHEAD** to become a human being?

In his own words *"Lord, now You are letting Your servant depart in peace, according to Your word; For my eyes have seen Your salvation"* What a powerful testimony of this old man. He could die now in peace. He saw what he asked from **GOD**, if he could only see this **SAVIOUR** coming to earth and

GOD gave him that promise and fulfilled it as well. Simon never knew that this specific morning as he walked through the pillars of the temple, he was an old man, between these pillars of Solomon that this **SAVIOUR** of the world will appear this specific morning. At the altar where the Leviticus priest offers, the noise of many people bringing their offers to the temple.

He didn't expect the baby that morning, but then appears this baby **JESUS**, and this old man was allowed to see **JESUS** and finishes his earthly tasks and then could say: "Now I can go in peace". You can die in peace. Isn't it true that death is the cut-off of all the friendships?

And it also means a companionship with **JESUS** forever. And with all these wonders coming with going to heaven. Think about it!

It is true, your friendships, your companionship with your wife or husband, your children, your family, your brothers and sisters, but mostly your mother and father. Your friends and work colleagues. Your circle of friends that is what death cuts you off from. But the other hand death brings you companionship with **JESUS HIMSELF**. And with all the wonderful people in heaven. Because being a child of **GOD** you greet all your family and friends at your death bed, and then the next moment when your spirit leaves your body, you get welcomened by the heavenly companions already in heaven.

Maybe your earthly friendships from earth continues in heaven, and with your purchase this **JESUS**, you know who will be there. See the **BIBLE** says in Heb 12 **JESUS** the **FATHER** and the **SPIRIT** of the perfect righteous. So that is true that all the earthly friendships will stop. But other friendships will continue in heaven, got to be a good reason. This is where a child of **GOD** can be happy at his death, as he wanted it whilst alive, after death he is happy because he goes to the ones already departed to heaven, his loved ones already there and meet up with them. That's why we always say "make sure you go to heaven, because I am coming soon to meet you there". We can die in the promises of the blood of **JESUS**; **HE** said **HE** is preparing this home, life after death for us. **GOD** always keeps **HIS** word and that is what we live and act on, **HIS WORD** as we know in the beginning was the **WORD** and the **WORD** was with **GOD** and the **WORD** was **GOD**. Even in the jaws of death **GOD** will carry us through.

When you open your eyes in the heavenly Jerusalem, you will be with ten thousands of Angels, arriving at the festival meeting ever held, at the firstborn souls, at **GOD** the judge, at the spirits of the righteous, at **JESUS** the mediator of the **NEW TESTAMENT**. The testament of the new alliance, the cross alliance, the blood alliance, **JESUS** who gave **HIS** life on the cross. That is what awaits you there in your dying hour. Ones a believer said softly in his dying moments and full of belief:

I am on the point where I have to meet death, I find the only mysterious baptise of Golgotha is the only thing I need now while I am meeting death. It must be very hard to approach death without **JESUS CHRIST**. Is death a jump into the dark?

Or is it a jump into **JESUS'S** arms? What's waiting on the other side for you?

Think again, are you jumping into the dark, or don't you know where you are going to? Or is it just a transfer to love protection to the one you love **JESUS CHRIST** my **LORD**? Maybe we should say like **JESUS** when **HE** prayed beforehand, and actually teaches us how to meet death. In Luk 23:46 **JESUS** said **HIS** last words before **HE** died: *"FATHER, into Your hands I commit My spirit."* And after **HE** said that **HE** breathed **HIS** last. Listen again **"Father into Your hands"**. What do you hear when you hear these words? Here hangs the **SON** of **GOD**, it is his dying hour. It is more than that, more than that **HIS** dying minute, **HIS** last seconds being in this earthly body. **HIS** last seconds in HIS body, trusting **HIS FATHER GOD**, the last words coming out of **HIS** mouth. **"Father into Your hands I commit My spirit."**

For **JESUS** the **FATHER** hand was the synonym of safety, strength and security. So death was a bonus for **JESUS**, there was security for **HIM** in death. When death cross your road how will you greet death? Will we greet death like a friend? Or will you greet death like an enemy? What are you saying? As a friend or an enemy? Now have you picked your answer? I am going to tell you what my answer is: I will greet death both ways. The **WORD** is clear in 1Cor 15 that the last hurdle we got to get over is death.

The last enemy, death is overcome in the last overcoming of death, where is your victory? The sting of death is sin. But **GOD** gives us the victory through **JESUS CHRIST**. The last enemy we have to beat is death. Surely it depends if you are prepared with a pure heart for the future awaiting us in heaven.

Then death comes like a friend who came to save you from the heavy life burdens. From you continuous fight against the devil, with sin and this world, and the trouble and how difficult our existence on earth could be. Sometimes the pain in your body.

If there were no preparation for death, it will come as an enemy. A Deadly enemy as well. Death steals you from blessings on the other side of the grave. You see for the believer who found true security at **JESUS**, death becomes the beaten at the place where we meet **JESUS CHRIST**.

JESUS said in Rev 1:17 & 18 *"And when I saw Him, I fell at His feet as dead. But He laid His right hand on me, saying to me, "Do not be afraid; I am the First and the Last. I am He who lives, and was dead, and behold, I am alive forevermore. Amen. And I have the keys of Hades and of Death."* When I die I meet the name face to face the victor over death, **JESUS CHRIST** who frees me of fearing death. Only in **HIM** death can be the following: Ps 116:15 says *"Precious in the sight of the LORD is the death of His saints."* You see it is not a tragic, like many come to the last hour before death with an unspeakable regret, when they have to face death.

Many learnt how to live and have a healthy live. They forgot to learn how to meet death, and **JESUS CHRIST** who free you from fearing death. Death and the fear and how to prepare. The scary death. A death threat in their hearts. It overcomes them, and their death is not joyful, to enter eternity. It does not exist by them. Their death is a root chopped death and they die without hope. Against the will the healthy dies, never learnt how to prepare for death. Remember what Moses said in Ps 90:10 *"The days of our lives are seventy years; and if by reason of strength they are eighty years, yet their boast is only labor and sorrow; for it is soon cut off, and we fly away."*

Verse 12 he says: *"So teach us to number our days, that we may gain a heart of wisdom."* Yes that is what Moses said: Teach us whilst we are on earth to gain a heart of wisdom to prepare to die. David said in Ps 23 *"Yea, though I walk through the valley of shadow of death, I will fear no evil; For You are with me; Your rod and Your staff, they comfort me."* A Child of **GOD** dies in peace. *"FATHER, into Your hands I commit My spirit."* Meditate on **GOD'S WORD**, look at **JESUS CHRIST**, look at **HIS** resurrection, look at **HIS** ascend to heaven and think how **HE** saves you against sin and death.

Now the last gate you enter before you receive your glorified body, listen to the voice of the **FATHER** calling you today to give your life to **HIM**. He formed us to praise and worship **HIM** forever. Readers please do it immediately! Now this day, this hour, this minute and this second before time tick its last tick. **GOD** didn't create us to burn in the pool of fire forever, where your body won't burn out and forever in pain. Forever in hell where there is no water, food, oxygen light, only darkness, no sleep and no rest. **Stop and think!** On the other side the **JESUS** side a fantastic lively site with your glorified resurrected body you will have freedom, love with **GOD** the **FATHER, JESUS** the **SON** and **HIS HOLY SPIRIT** forever every second.

FATHER through **JESUS** I come to you this instant without a second passing by and thank YOU that nothing will hold me back from rising to YOU and not even death can hold me back. I ask YOU to take me and wash me whiter than snow to fit in YOUR garments for the glorified body you promised me and to be ready when YOUR angels take me to YOU forever. I Thank YOU for this promise. AMEN

BIBLE References:

Ps 9:10
Amos 4:12
Luk 2: 29 & 30
Luk 23:46
1 Cor 15
Rev 1:17 & 18
Ps 116:15
Ps 90:10,12

Notes:

Chapter 12
What should I do now and how should I stay

I rush myself to give just the right information through to you, what to do now after the **HOLY SPIRIT** *gave me; through* **GOD'S SPIRIT** *how to stay in order to please the* **FATHER** *to gain eternal life. Through the book I could just put some importance on scriptures from the* **BIBLE** *to support you with your growth, but the best growth for the believer is to keep working through the* **BIBLE** *with* **GOD'S SPIRIT** *that unlocks everything for you, the absolute teacher.*

Most new converts ask the question, what should I do now? Mat 16:24-28 *"Then Jesus said to His disciples, "If anyone desires to come after Me, let him deny himself, and take up his cross, and follow Me. For whoever desires to save his life will lose it, but whoever loses his life for My sake will find it. For what profit is it to a man if he gains the whole world, and loses his own soul? Or what will a man give in exchange for his soul? For the Son of Man will come in the glory of His Father with His angels, and then He will reward each according to his works. "Assuredly, I say to you, there are some standing here who shall not taste death till they see the Son of Man coming in His kingdom."* What does it mean what JESUS said to them? , *"If anyone desires to come after Me,* "We surely know now what JESUS spoke about after we have worked through all the chapters in this book! It is after eternal life when HE fetches us. The next question, what does it mean to deny yourself? It does not mean to be worthy of ourselves and then to trust CHRIST rather who is GOD. And to give HIM the opportunity to make decisions from the moment I accepted him.

Now what does the following mean? *"and take up his cross".* It is obvious to take yourself, your whole existence, your body and everything that has to do with you, either bad or good.

You take your entire package leave nothing behind, that can hold you back and you take everything on your shoulders.

Mat 11:30 *"For MY yoke is easy and MY burden is light."* So we admit that JESUS starts to carry our burdens from that instant. Now what does the next means? *"and follow Me.* "You stop in your path as you walk now and start immediately following JESUS on the narrow road to eternal heaven with HIM. Also in Matthew 11 we read about JESUS's yoke. Mat 11:28 to 30 *"Come to Me, all you who labor and are heavy laden, and I will give you rest. Take My yoke upon you and learn from Me, for I am gentle and lowly in heart, and you will find rest for your souls."* Read the following 1 Pet 4:1&2 *"Therefore, since*

Christ suffered for us in the flesh, arm yourselves also with the same mind, for he who has suffered in the flesh has ceased from sin, that he no longer should live the rest of his time in the flesh for the lusts of men, but for the will of GOD." Please read the entire chapter of 1 Pet 4. The **WORD** of **GOD** teaches us in Mat 6:20 & 21 *"but lay up for yourselves treasures in heaven, where neither moth nor rust destroys and where thieves do not break in and steal. For where your treasure is, there your heart will be also."* In order to strengthen the new character you are building now, you must learn to do certain things to get you ready to go after **JESUS**. Gal 5:1 *"Stand fast therefore in the liberty by which Christ has made us free, and do not be entangled again with a yoke of bondage."*

And verse 13 *"For you, brethren, have been called to liberty; only do not use liberty as an opportunity for the flesh, but through love serve one another."* The love that Paul refers to here brings us back to the **OLD TESTAMENT** in Exodus 20:1 to 17 the commandments of the **LORD**. Believe me if all people knew the **GODLY** ten commandments, and also to live to follow that, and the most important one *"Thou shalt love thy neighbour as thyself."* No wonder Paul wrote to the Ephesians in Eph 5:1&2 *"Therefore be imitators of God as dear children. And walk in love, as Christ also has loved us and given Himself for us, an offering and a sacrifice to God for a sweet-smelling aroma."*

The **BIBLE** is full of the love of **JESUS** and **GOD**, because **GOD** is love. Furthermore, we must hold onto **GOD'S** armor. We read in EFE 6:10 to 18 *"Finally, my brethren, be strong in the Lord and in the power of His might. Put on the whole armor of God, that you may be able to stand against the wiles of the devil. For we do not wrestle against flesh and blood, but against principalities, against powers, against the rulers of the darkness of this age, against spiritual hosts of wickedness in the heavenly places. Therefore take up the whole armor of God, that you may be able to withstand in the evil day, and having done all, to stand. Stand therefore, having girded your waist with truth, having put on the breastplate of righteousness, and having shod your feet with the preparation of the gospel of peace; above all, taking the shield of faith with which you will be able to quench all the fiery darts of the wicked one. And take the helmet of salvation, and the sword of the Spirit, which is the word of God; praying always with all prayer and supplication in the Spirit, being watchful to this end with all perseverance and supplication for all the saints—"* As we were taught praying and speaking with **GOD'S SPIRIT** who lives in us is our stronghold. You might need to request my module about prayer and vasting.

There is a promise, one of many in **GOD'S WORD** in Mat 7:11 *"If you then, being evil, know how to give good gifts to your children, how much more will your Father who is in heaven give good things to those who ask Him!"* Also in Phil 2:9 to 11 *"Therefore God also has highly exalted Him and given Him the name which is above every name, that at the name of Jesus every knee should bow, of those in heaven, and of those on* *earth, and of those under the earth, and that every tongue should confess that Jesus Christ is Lord, to the glory of God the Father."*

This brings us to the final section **how to stay**. **JESUS** says everything to you in Matthew 5, 6 7 what we must do and be immutable in faith. In love which is the greatest and humility. Not only humble for humans but humble before **GOD** because **GOD** gives life.

The rich man asked **JESUS** a very good question in Luk 18:18 to 24 Teaches us that one should think carefully when there is an opportunity for you to follow **JESUS** and there are human things that prevent you from following **HIM**. Please read the complete section.

But in Luk 18:24 *"And when Jesus saw that he became very sorrowful, He said, how hard it is for those who have riches to enter the kingdom of God!"* With this section, we do not make a profit decision to take everything and sell and throw everything up and follow **JESUS**. But Jesus knows because **HE** is **GOD**, that we as human beings are sometimes attached to earthly or more to our earthly possessions than to return to **GOD** in **HIS** house. We forget that **HE** is the provider. Many verse sections refer us that we have to gather rewards in the right place. Please read Luk 12 the concerns of life, how **JESUS** explains things.

Verse 31 is another thing that stands out for us **how should I stay!** *"But seek the kingdom of God, and all these things shall* *be added to you."* And further 1 Cor 6:9 *"Do you not know that the unrighteous will not inherit the kingdom of God? Do not be deceived. Neither fornicators, nor idolaters, nor adulterers, nor homosexuals, nor sodomites,"* verse 20 *"For you were bought at a price; therefore glorify God in your body and in your spirit, which are God's."* Here is the question again "**how should I stay?** With this writing, as every human being wants, I humbly want to make every human being aware of today's facts that turn the evil forces for us as a man to mind and all of them lack the kingdom of **GOD** and that's why we must steer ourselves away from us, and roll away **JESUS'S** grave stone wheel to see that he is no longer there, but risen and **HE** lives in us and in our hearts.

Now we can make the distinction when we see the eclipse and do not turn our head away from it but in our minds see the distinction. Now important facts: People say its right to do the following: You may use alcohol because **JESUS** has made wine. People do not bluff yourselves! They say it's also right to smoke and do drugs and things like that, because it's not addictive!

And we must get tattoos and put rings in our body! Stop for a moment, it's that how **GOD** created us? Let us go back to the previous section of the **WORD** of **GOD**. Verse 20 says clearly *"For you were bought at a price; therefore glorify God in your body and in your spirit, which are God's."*

How dare you as human being tear parts of **GOD'S WORD** away and think that you will not be punished? Remember what Mat

6:24 say: *"No one can serve two masters; for either he will hate the one and love the other, or else he will be loyal to the one and despise the other. You cannot serve God and mammon."* We also read in the letter in Rev 3:1 to 6 but take note what **GOD** says in verse 6 *"And to the angel of the church in Sardis write, these things says He who has the seven Spirits of God and the seven stars: "I know your works, that you have a name that you are alive, but you are dead. Be watchful, and strengthen the things which remain, that are ready to die, for I have not found your works perfect before God. Remember therefore how you have received and heard; hold fast and repent. Therefore if you will not watch, I will come upon you as a thief, and you will not know what hour I will come upon you. You have a few names even in Sardis who have not defiled their garments; and they shall walk with Me in white, for they are worthy. He who overcomes shall be clothed in white garments, and I will not blot out his name from the Book of Life; but I will confess his name before My Father and before His angels. "He who has an ear, let him hear what the Spirit says to the churches."*

Then the promise in verse 5 *"He who overcomes shall be clothed in white garments, and I will not blot out his name from the Book of Life; but I will confess his name before My Father and before His angels."* So we stay "what should I do now?" Read in Ps 95:1&2 *"Oh come, let us sing to the LORD! Let us shout joyfully to the Rock of our salvation. Let us come before His presence with thanksgiving; Let us shout joyfully to Him with psalms."*

What should I do now and how should I stay | 181

Thousands of people and we are part of it, sit on sports fields and stadiums and scream and clap hands for our sports heroes, but we're too embarrassed to scream for our **GOD** with praise and hymns. People think about this is true. What do you do to praise **GOD**? In Ps 95:7 *"For He is our God, and we are the people of His pasture, and the sheep of His hand. Today, if you will hear His voice:"* We also read in James when we need wisdom; we know where to find it. Prov 2:6 *"For the LORD gives wisdom; from His mouth come knowledge and understanding;"*

Also in Jam 1:5&6 *"If any of you lacks wisdom, let him ask of God, who gives to all liberally and without reproach, and it will be given to him. But let him ask in faith, with no doubting, for he who doubts is like a wave of the sea driven and tossed by the wind."*

Just believe with humility and the **SPIRIT** of **GOD** is faithful to give you the necessary insight and wisdom in **HIS WORD**, to keep you on track and to help others get along or stay on the right track. People must not be relaxed or lazy because we are warned in **GOD'S WORD** in certain places not to be lukewarm. Rev 3:16 *"So then, because you are lukewarm, and neither cold nor hot, I will vomit you out of My mouth."* Persevere in your decision **'What should I do now'** to get eternal life. This brings me to the end of this book.

END

Gal 5:22 to 25 *"But the fruit of the Spirit is love, joy, peace, longsuffering, kindness, goodness, faithfulness, gentleness, self-control. Against such there is no law. And those who are Christ's have crucified the flesh with its passions and desires. If we live in the Spirit, let us also walk in the Spirit."*

1 Cor 15:57 & 58 *"But thanks be to God, who gives us the victory through our Lord Jesus Christ. Therefore, my beloved brethren, be steadfast, immovable, always abounding in the work of the Lord, "AND NOW ABIDE FAITH, HOPE, LOVE, THESE THREE; BUT THE GREATEST OF THESE IS LOVE."*

1 Cor 13:13

Final prayer with steps

FATHER here I am giving you all the honors and I give myself to YOU right now without anyone except YOUR SPIRIT convincing me to do so.

I now know that I can come just as I am and that YOU now forgive my sins and that YOU wash it away with JESUS'S death on the cross, through the BLOOD of JESUS and never thinking about it again. Bind my spirit now FATHER through YOUR HOLY SPIRIT to renew my mind to work on my new life after death. FATHER put me in your house of GOD where I can work with your congregation to make me stronger in YOUR work to fight evil when the darkness wants to attack me.

I'm asking it now on my knees in humility before you in JESUS' NAME, which is the only MEDIATOR to GOD the FATHER.

Amen.

BIBLE References:

Mat 16:24-28

Mat 11:28 to 30

1 Pet 4:1&2

Mat 6:20 & 21

Gal 5:1

Exodus 20:1 to 17

Eph 5: 1 & 2

Eph 6:10 to 18

Mat 7:11

Phil 2:9 to 11

Luk 18:18 to 24

1 Cor 6:9

Mat 6: 24

Rev 3: 1 to 6

Ps 95:1 & 2

Rev 3: 1 to 6

Ps 95:7

Prov 2:6

Jam 1:5 & 6

Rev 3:16

Gal 5:22 to 25

1 Cor 15:57 & 58

Notes:

www.ingramcontent.com/pod-product-compliance
Lightning Source LLC
Chambersburg PA
CBHW071922290426
44110CB00013B/1447